Be Your Own Tactics C

Dedicated to my Dad,
the bravest man I know.

Be Your Own Tactics Coach

BY JON EMMETT

John Wiley & Sons, Ltd

Registered office
John Wiley & Sons Ltd, The Atrium, Southern Gate, Chichester, West Sussex, PO19 8SQ,
United Kingdom

Editorial office
For details of our global editorial offices, for customer services and for information about how to apply for
permission to reuse the copyright material in this book please see our website at www.wiley.com

Wiley also publishes its books in a variety of electronic formats and by print-on-demand. Some content that
appears in standard print versions of this book may not be available in other formats. For more information
about Wiley products, visit us at www.wiley.com

Designations used by companies to distinguish their products are often claimed as trademarks. All brand
names and product names used in this book are trade names, service marks, trademarks or registered
trademarks of their respective owners. The publisher is not associated with any product or vendor
mentioned in this book. This publication is designed to provide accurate and authoritative information in
regard to the subject matter covered. It is sold on the understanding that the publisher is not engaged in
rendering professional services. If professional advice or other expert assistance is required, the services of
a competent professional should be sought.

Library of Congress Cataloging-in-Publication Data
Emmett, Jon.
　　Be your own tactics coach/by Jon Emmett.
　　　p.　cm.
　　ISBN: 978-0-470-97321-9
　　　1. Sailing.　I. Title.
　　GV811.E485　2011
　　797.124--dc22

A catalogue record for this book is available from the British Library.

ISBN 978-0-470-97321-9 (pbk); ISBN 978-1-119-95134-6 (ebk)
ISBN 978-1-119-95135-3 (ebk); ISBN 978-1-119-95136-0 (ebk)

Wiley Nautical – sharing your passion.

At Wiley Nautical we're passionate about anything that happens in, on or around the water.

Wiley Nautical used to be called Fernhurst Books and was founded by a national and European sailing
champion. Our authors are the leading names in their fields with Olympic gold medals around their
necks and thousands of sea miles in their wake. Wiley Nautical is still run by people with a love of
sailing, motorboating, surfing, diving, kitesurfing, canal boating and all things aquatic.

Set in Futura 10/15 by MPS Limited, a Macmillan Company, Chennai, India
Printed in Great Britain by Butler Tanner & Dennis, Somerset

Contents

Introduction

As with the original title, *Be Your Own Sailing Coach*, the aim is to produce a book that is very user friendly, meaning you really can get the most out of it by putting in the minimum of effort and just reading the sections you need to.

To make the book even more accessible each chapter has been divided into three sections with Beginner, Intermediate and Advanced tactics (for example Chapter 5: 5.1 Basic Tacking, 5.2 Tacking to Loose Cover, 5.3 Tacking to Tight Cover). This makes it easy for people new to racing to get the basic concepts, whilst more advanced racers can go straight to the information they need without having to wade through lots of stuff they are already very familiar with.

Top class sailing is all about that extra final percent, but you need to get the basics right as well. You can race extremely well by just getting the "big" things right (always sailing the right way up the beat etc.) before you worry about "smaller" things (which side to position yourself to your main opposition). It is definitely worth mentioning that you should not allow the smaller things (covering the opposition) to override the bigger issue (which way to go up the beat) or both you and your closest opposition could end up having a bad result (although in some cases this *may* be what you desire). Just remember whatever is going on, and don't forget the basics.

Just like improving any aspect of your sailing you need to be focused. Before delving into the book I would suggest you fill out the dartboard at the back, as you did for *Be Your Own Sailing Coach*, to make sure you are working on the areas that will help you improve the most. You can then go and practise these tactics or at least be more aware of them when you train or just during your club race.

To make it easy to remember, the boat's "surname" has been designed to give an indication as to how they are sailing. For example: Finlay Footing likes to sail the boat fast and free and you may be able to identify yourself as him or someone you race against as like him. This will explain what your best option is and how to deal with him or her. Please note the names represent the helm/tactician and are therefore male and female (although all boats are of course female).

There is a full index of all the characters in the back of the book. Each boat has its own distinct colour.

Chapter 1
Pre Start

Basic Preparations
Spotting the Changes
Those Final Few Minutes

1.1   Basic Preparations

Before you even decide to enter the race/regatta make sure you are properly prepared. How long does it take to the venue? (Giving you enough rest.) Have you sorted out good accommodation? When do you need to enter? (Many regattas implement a surcharge if you enter late, so make your mind up!) Is your boat race ready and do you have all the spares you need?

Read the sailing instructions so you know the course you are racing, where it is and when, and don't forget to check the official notice board for changes to the SIs (sailing instructions) as it is not uncommon for amendments to be made. World Championships have been won and lost when people didn't notice a change of start time.

Races can be won and lost before the warning signal is even blown. The key thing is to establish what the most important tactic(s) will be for the day. Get the big things sorted (like not overstanding the layline with strong current under you) before you worry about the little things (a small amount of dirty air).

You need to break things down so first of all consider the course you would sail in the absence of other boats.

Examples:

A strong favourable current (or less adverse current) on one side of the course may be the most important factor, especially with slower moving boats. You can check the current by placing a 2/3 full bottle of liquid by a mark and seeing how far it moves in a minute.

If the wind is offshore you can check the current on your sail out to the start line. Launch early to give yourself plenty of time.

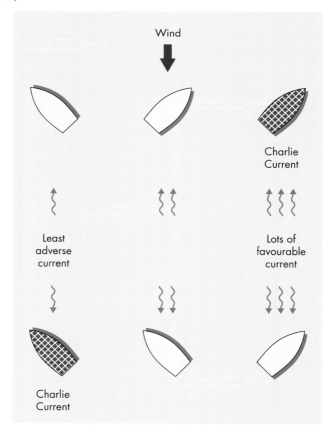

1.1a Charlie Current is always keen to maximise his tidal advantage compared to other boats

If there is a big shift, getting to it first can make a real difference. You may be expecting this windshift because of a weather forecast or if the wind is stable you may see the shift affecting boats further to windward or there may be a wind bend due to the shore line.

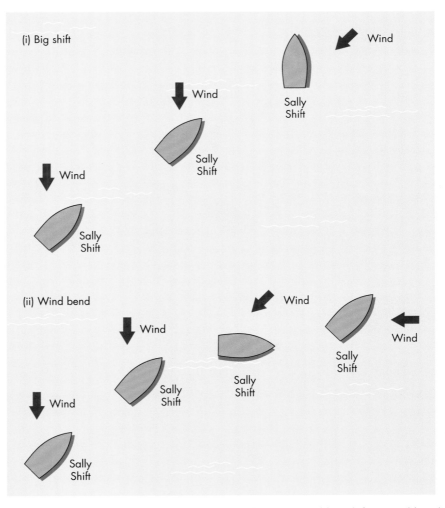

1.1b Sally Shift is always keen to maximise the gain of an expected big shift (i) wind bend (ii)

With a big difference in wind speed the windier side of the course may be heavily favoured, especially with boats which plane upwind. More wind makes the water look darker, then when the water is dark there is more wind where there are more white horses. In light winds (under 7 knots) even a small difference in wind speed (say 4–6 knots) can make a big difference in boatspeed.

If the breeze is offshore you can probably work out which is the windiest part of the race course on the way to the start line.

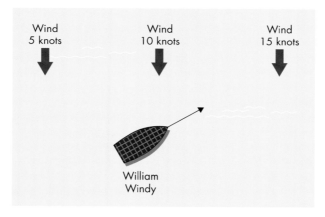

1.1c William Windy is always off to the windiest part of the race course to help his boat go faster

Get out early and if there is an oscillation try and get in tune with it (work out the frequency and duration). If not just practise your tacking!!

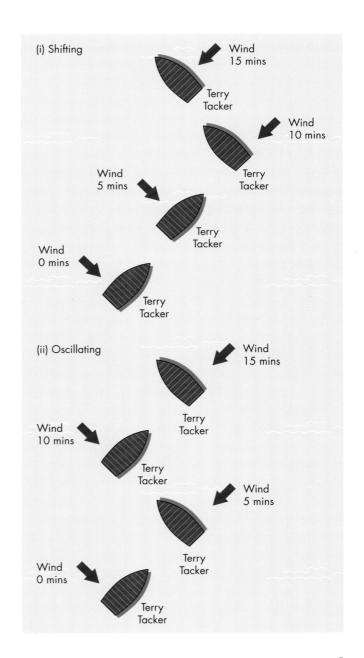

1.1d Terry Tacker tacking in a (i) shifting and (ii) oscillating breeze

Lastly, don't forget good boatwork is essential. To look at the more technical side (before you even hit the water) see chapters 4 and 20 in *Be Your Own Sailing Coach*.

1.2 Spotting the Changes

Wind awareness is key (especially in light winds). Ensure you pay careful attention to changes in wind strength (darker or lighter patches on the water for stronger/lighter areas of wind) and shifts (which are often the key reason for tacking (See Chapters 3 Upwind and 4 The First Beat). By having a good look before the start you should know what to expect (but you will still need to keep your head out of the boat).

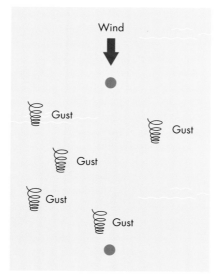

1.2a There would appear to be more wind on the left hand side of the race course

You can also expect changes in current. Now obviously you do not have time to drop a tide stick in during a race but you can make observations such as how the current is affecting you (using transits) and examining any buoys you pass. The buoys will appear to be travelling towards the current with a small amount of slack water behind the buoy (pointing the way the current is going). The faster the buoys appear to be going (the more bow waves at the front and the greater the slack water behind) the stronger the current. Hence you can see if the current is increasing or decreasing and if there is any change in direction.

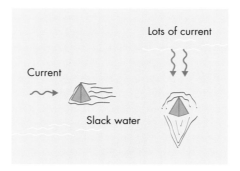

1.2b The effect of current on a buoy

There may also be expected changes in the wind direction. For example if there is a sea breeze (in the northern hemisphere) you would expect the mean wind direction to go to the right (the wind can still be shifty with a sea breeze). So make sure you know what a header is and what a lift is. If you are sailing at 180 degrees in the morning for example, this might be a lift, while in the afternoon if you are sailing at 180 degrees this could now be a header.

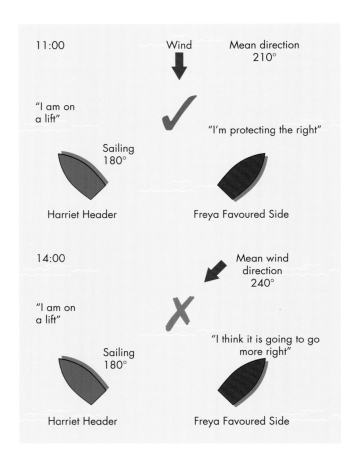

1.3 Those Final Few Minutes

Those final few minutes are absolutely crucial. In fact in some ways the results of the race can be decided before it has even begun! This is not the time to be simply reaching around enjoying the breeze. . .

So the most important thing is to focus. Time often has a variable quality. While you are waiting for the race committee to start the sequence, time may seem to drag but the last minute can absolutely fly by and you suddenly find yourself over or further behind the line than you hoped.

Remember sailing is a non contact sport! And the racing rules start from the preparatory signal (the rules still apply but there is no penalty for breaking them). However you must not interfere with a boat who is already racing. You are technically racing when one preparatory signal has gone. You should be awake from the warning signal, looking for information about the race, but at the preparatory signal you should be 100% focused – after all you are now racing!

The rules state that at the preparatory signal your boat should be afloat (I know a few club racers who tend to launch at the preparatory signal). You want to check the starting penalty as this will affect how you approach the start. Examples are: the black flag (you are disqualified if you are over the start line with a minute or less to go); the Z flag (you have 20% of the number of boats in the fleet added to your score if you are over the start line with a minute or less to go); I flag (you are disqualified if you are over with a minute or less to go unless you return to the pre-start side of the course going around the ends of the line) or no penalty (you simply need to dip back behind the line if you were over at the starting signal).

Remember whether you get a good start or not is only clear about 10 seconds after the start. So keep going. That boat which is about to roll/leebow you may hit a wave and stop allowing you to break through.

Your build up to the start of the first race of the day (for a race of around an hour) should be something like this:

Time to start	Focus
60 minutes*	Check and double check your boat and launch, checking the conditions on your way out. Register with the committee boat if needed (in some regattas you have to show your sail number on entering the racing area).
50 minutes	Do a practice beat. You don't have to do the whole thing but you need to be comfortable that you know which way you want to go.
30 minutes	Downwind boat handling. Practise a kite hoist and gybe and then pack the kite on the correct side for the first hoist in the race.

(continued)

20 minutes	Double check the rig set up – are you expecting the wind to drop or increase? Is the beat still the same as it was 30 minutes ago? If not, what is changing?
10 minutes	Check out the start line and keep checking. Depending upon the regatta the warning signal may go now.
5 minutes	Now into starting sequence – so focus!

*Assumes onshore wind, otherwise you will need to allow more time to get to the starting area.

In the final minute it is crucial that you are in the correct area of the line as shown in 1.3 a.

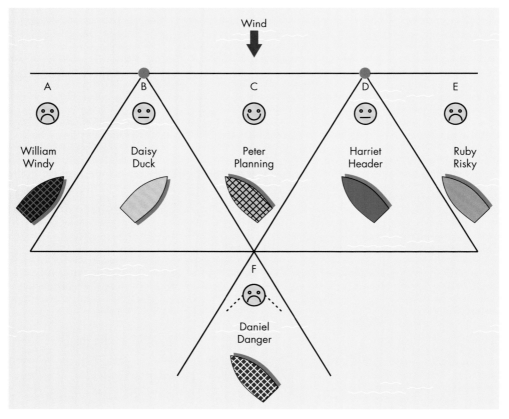

1.3 a Where to be with one minute to go

Area	Reason	Happy?	Options
A	William Windy was on the left side of the course then the wind died and he could not get back to the starting area.	Sad	Not only does he have to duck any starboard tackers, he must also keep clear of the leeward boats in B as he is windward boat.
B	Daisy Duck has left coming into the starting area a bit late but all is not lost.	Not happy	She should be able to duck a few boats and get to the line. She just has to pray a gap opens up!
C	Peter Planning is in the triangle that means he can definitely cross the line. If right was favoured he would be further to the right; if left was favoured he would be further to the left.	Happy	Peter Planning can look for a gap and start where he wants.
D	Harriet Header got the wind wrong. She thought she was on the layline to the start line but she was above it.	Not happy	If she can see a gap further down the line she should get in it asap. Otherwise she has to stay up and clear of the leeward boats in C hoping a gap opens up, or stay where she is and tack for clear air as soon as the boats in C have started.
E	Ruby Risky thought a gap was going to open up by the committee boat but it didn't. There is now a whole queue of boats in the waiting area hoping to start by the committee boat.	Sad	If there is a gap go for it. Otherwise stay clear and hope the boats are drifting fast. She will have to wait for those boats in C and D to start. She can then go behind them and tack to the right, hoping not too many people have already done this.
F	Daniel Danger was way too late getting out to the starting area and will probably miss the start.	Very sad (crying his eyes out)	Hope for a general recall!!!

Chapter 2
Starts

Line Bias

Big Fleet Starts

Knowing your Rights

2.1 Line Bias

You must continually check the bias of the line as it can change. Remember if the line bias is two boat lengths, that equals three boat lengths sailing (as we don't sail head to wind!) Therefore do not stray too far away from what you consider to be the favoured end with ten minutes to go. Remember that from your pre-start strategy you may have decided you must go one way upwind. This means you may choose to start away from the most upwind end of the line if it makes it easier to go where you want. Ensure you have accurate timing: check this at the 5, 4 and 1 minute.

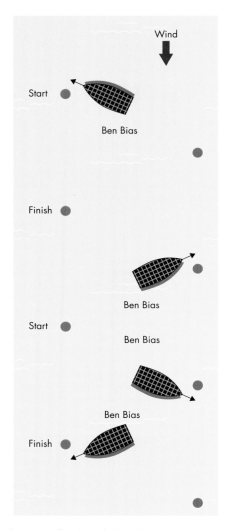

2.1a Line bias favoured end to start/finish with Ben Bias

Remember if you are finishing going upwind through the start line then the favoured end of the finish line is the opposite end to the favoured end of the start line, assuming nothing has changed during the course of the race. Remember any part of the boat can be over: it is simply the part which is most upwind. In other words if you are in the middle of the boat on the line, then you are half a boat length over. . .

Starting in the middle of the line (more than 25% from either end) it is harder to judge where the line is (as you are further from the ends). Here a good transit is essential to avoid the mid line sag which could be several boat lengths on a long line.

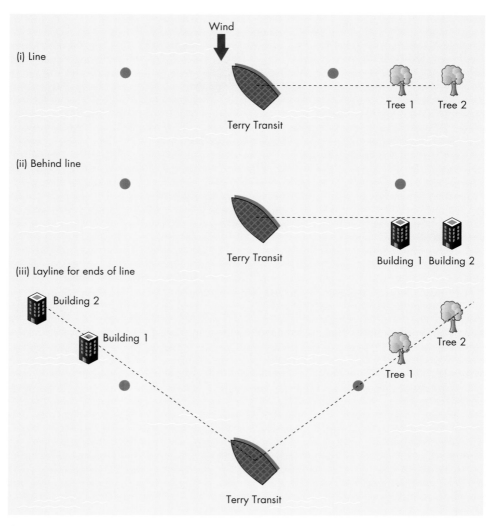

2.1b Transits with Terry Transit (i) line (ii) behind line (iii) layline for ends of the line (iv) middle of the line

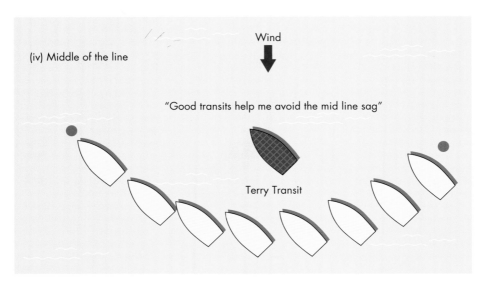

(iv) Middle of the line

Wind

"Good transits help me avoid the mid line sag"

Terry Transit

2.1b (Continued)

You also need to consider the course bias (which way you would go up the course). You would really worry if the course were offset if the course was very small and/or you were likely to end up over the laylines. In the absence of other factors you would want to start next to the end of the line which was the most upwind, not that which was closest to the first mark (remember boats do not sail head to wind). It is usually easier to judge your position on the line nearer an end.

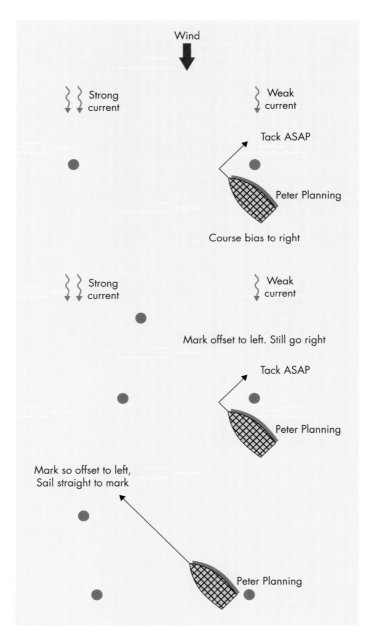

2.1c Peter Planning considers the course bias

Finally check out how long it takes you to get up to full speed. Remember the wind and waves at start time can be confused making it harder to accelerate. Talk everything through with the people you sail with and have a few dummy runs.

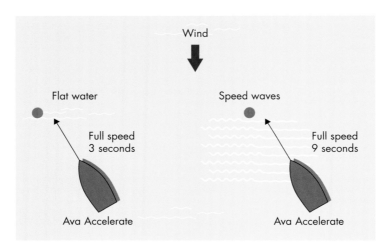

2.1d Ava Accelerate gets up to full speed

2.2 Big Fleet Starts

Although many international fleets will sail round robins or have restricted entries, meaning fleet numbers are smaller, there are still plenty of national regattas which have long start lines (perhaps taking five minutes to sail down). So it is well worth getting the tactics right, because starting in big fleets is one of the most difficult skills to master as it is hard to practise (there are a limited number of big fleet starts for each class, each year).

Good starting in big fleets is one of the best ways to raise your game. If you can come off the line in the first ten boats then you are already in a secure position, on the "escalator" to the windward mark. Meanwhile the rest of the boats who are sitting in dirty air or sailing on the wrong tack (considering the biggest factor for example being on the lifting tack) are effectively stepping down the "escalator".

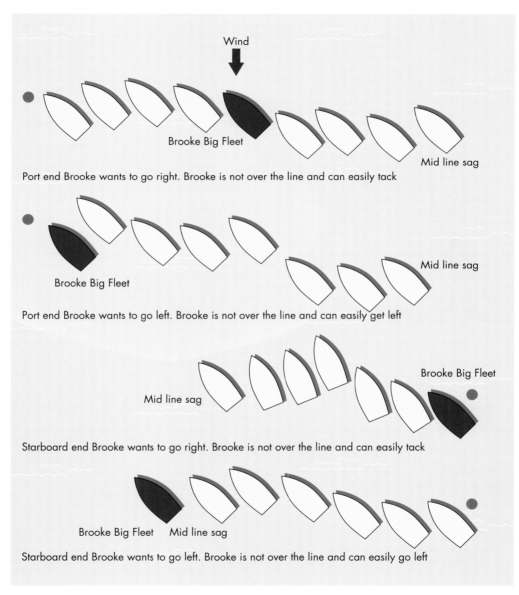

2.2a A big fleet start with Brooke Big Fleet

Winning the end can be very important. For a port end favoured line the port tack approach can work very well to control the fleet.

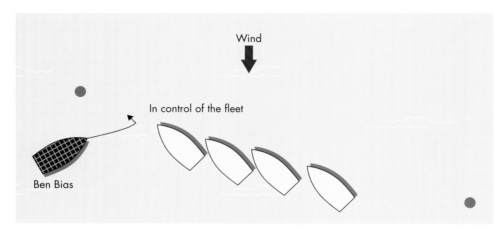

2.2b Port tack approach with Ben Bias

For a starboard favoured line we need to position ourselves up drift of the favoured end so as we gradually drift down the line we end up in the perfect place at start time. After all, life is all about being in the right place at the right time. If the starboard end is a large committee boat you may wish to start a boat length or two away from it, if it is producing a large wind shadow.

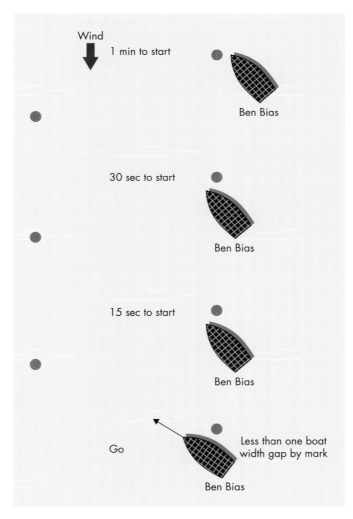

Wind

1 min to start

Ben Bias

30 sec to start

Ben Bias

15 sec to start

Ben Bias

Go

Less than one boat
width gap by mark

Ben Bias

2.2c Drift with Ben Bias

For an even line and perhaps one where you are not sure which way you want to go (or it is a shifty day and you just want to keep your options open) start towards the middle of the line. Then move down to the line either coming from behind and then luffing up into a gap or sailing down on port and tacking under someone with a good gap.

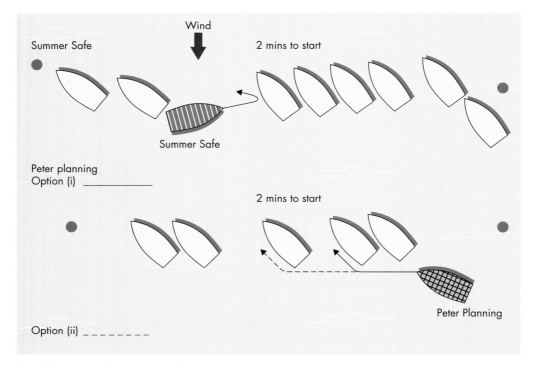

2.2d Summer Safe and Peter Planning option (i) and option (ii)

2.3   Knowing your Rights

Knowing your rights at start time is absolutely crucial. It is not simply he (or she) who shouts loudest who has right of way (and there are few places on the race course which have as much shouting as the start line). I still hear people shouting "mast abeam", a term which has not been in the rules for many, many years!

In a perfect world you would simply find your space and at the appropriate time accelerate like Ava Accelerate (see 2.1d); however this is not always possible. So we may end up having to tack in like Ben Bias. Remember there is no proper course before the start. After the start line if you did not approach from behind (Ben Bias tacked in) you may luff up to head to wind as long as the other boats can keep clear. This is why it is good to tack underneath someone rather than come in from behind – it gives you more options.

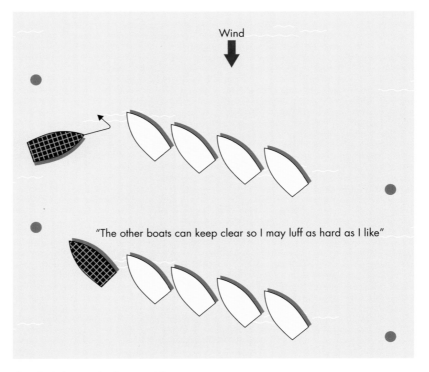

Wind

"The other boats can keep clear so I may luff as hard as I like"

2.3a Ben Bias's rights as the leeward boat

If however you are looking to start at the starboard end you will most likely have boats to leeward of you. You must keep clear of these. However they must give you room to keep clear. (They can not simply sail in about 1 cm from your boat and expect you to be able to keep clear.)

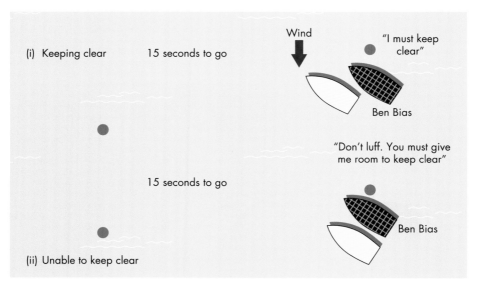

2.3b Ben Bias's rights as the windward boat (i) keeping clear, (ii) unable to keep clear

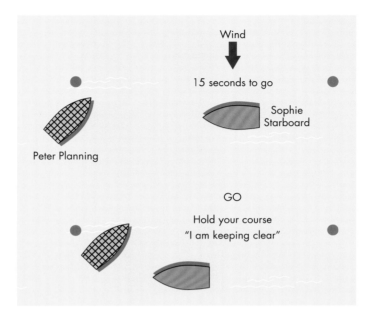

2.3c Peter Planning on port meets Sophie Starboard on starboard

This is a key idea where the right of way boat must give the give way boat room to keep clear. Here Peter Planning has lined up for a port flyer: he is keeping clear of Sophie Starboard who holds her course, as if she changed her course Peter Planning would not be able to keep clear.

Chapter 3
Upwind

Basic Upwind Sailing

Dealing with the Conditions

When to Tack

3.1   Basic Upwind Sailing

When you are sailing upwind your goal is to minimise the amount of time it takes you to get to the windward mark. It is not to maximise your speed (you could reach around all day and make no progress upwind) nor is it to point as close as possible to the wind (as you will end up going very slowly).

However it is possible to sail a range of angles and still make equally good progress upwind as demonstrated by Finlay Footing and Poppy Pinching

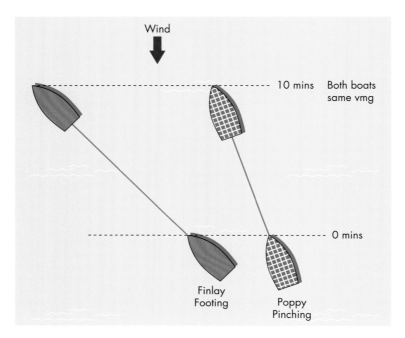

Wind

10 mins   Both boats same vmg

0 mins

Finlay
Footing

Poppy
Pinching

3.1a Finlay Footing and Poppy Pinching

However in terms of ease of getting to the windward mark somewhere in between is usually easier as it is easier to sail to. The problem with Finlay (Footing) is that you can easily lose high for no extra speed and the problem with Poppy (Pinching) is that you can easily lose speed trying to stay high. Being in the middle you are less likely to make an error as you can sail slightly higher or lower and still maintain maximum velocity made good (vmg). It will also probably be easier to hold your lane as this is likely to be the angle most other boats are sailing at.

However there are times when footing is very good: to get across to one side of the race course, perhaps to roll over another boat (get to windward and give them dirty air) or to get to a favoured side of the course for example out of bad current, into stronger wind or to be the first person into the new shift.

Likewise pinching has its place: if you want to stay away from one side of the course (it is a shifty day and you want to stay in the middle of the course) or perhaps to stay out of adverse tide or to leebow another boat.

So for example if you have been on starboard lift for a long time you may tend to pinch on starboard tack so as not to get too far away from the centre of the course and then as soon as the port lift comes in foot on port tack to get back over to the centre of the course as quickly as possible.

This also means you cross the other boats as soon as possible (you have not secured any gain to windward unless you are directly to windward as if the wind shifts again towards the other boats they gain on you – so if the wind went to the right the boats on the right would gain).

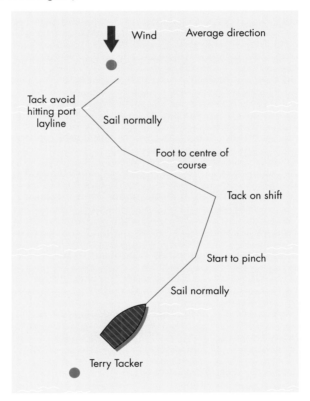

3.1b Staying central in the race course with Terry Tacker

Whether you pinch or foot may be related to the weight of the crew (it is easier for heavier crews to foot, especially in strong winds and it is easier for light crews to pinch, especially in light winds) or to the rig set up. For more information see chapter 11 in *Be Your Own Sailing Coach.*

3.2   Dealing with the Conditions

What is the wind like today? Is it steady in wind speed and direction, or is it constantly changing?

In light winds avoid too much leeward heel. This may make it feel as if you have more power, but it will increase the drag. Instead move your weight forward to decrease drag. This will also give you more feel on the rudder, helping you to steer more accurately for changes in wind speed and direction. Remember in really light winds pressure is king as it will not only help you to go faster but you will also point higher (as your sails and foils become more efficient.)

In medium winds you can now get the boat up to full speed. So the best plan is usually to get the boat up to full speed first and then you can aim for pointing (turning additional power into height). If you try and pinch first you risk stalling the sails and it will most likely take longer to get to maximum velocity made good (vmg). Remember if your boat planes to windward then in theory there is no maximum vmg!!!

In strong winds you are really looking to depower the rig (see chapter 11 in *Be Your Own Sailing Coach* for explanations on flattening sails, raking the mast and inducing leech twist). Sailing in strong winds is difficult, so you need to make it as easy as possible. Hike/trapeze as hard as you can consistently and keep the steering smooth. Keep the boat completely flat and make sure you use good equipment (old sails are likely to be stretched, old masts will have poorer gust response etc.).

In gusty conditions the wind will usually be very unstable (there is a lot of mixing with the stronger winds coming down) or shifty (where they are affected by coming over a land mass, especially hills, mountains etc.).

Gusts are usually clearly visible on the water but they come in different shapes and sizes: sometimes long thin streaks where the wind has funnelled between buildings, and sometimes large cat paws where the wind has come down from above and is spreading out.

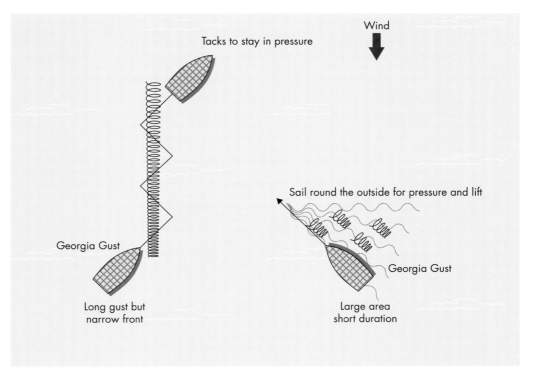

3.2a Georgia Gust works different gusts type: long and thin, fat and wide

If you are in a boat which planes upwind, gusts can be especially useful as there will be a clear speed advantage if you can maximise your time spent in stronger winds. You just need to weigh up whether it is worth sailing more distance for the extra speed you get if you get to the gust. The key is to get your head out of the boat and see if there is a pattern, perhaps more gusts on one side of the course.

When going upwind you will of course have a greater frequency of gusts as you are sailing towards the wind. You need to set your boat up to achieve the highest average speed. Depending upon the frequency of the gusts this means being underpowered in the lulls, perfectly set up for the mean wind and slightly overpowered in the gusts. However the more frequent the gusts, the closer your rig will be optimised for them.

The harder the conditions (big slamming gusts) the more you need to make your boat easy to sail (perhaps playing the sheet more or sailing with a softer leach) as you can lose a great deal if the boat stalls, and even more if you end up going for a swim.

Remember the bigger the area of the gust (with more dark water with a bigger gust) the longer it will last, and the faster it approaches the greater the wind speed. Depending upon where the gust comes from it may also affect the wind direction as follows:

Boat on Starboard tack

Gust from	Action
Front	Header
Right	Lifting
Left	Big header

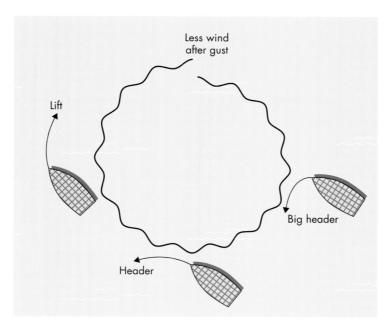

3.2b Georgia surrounded by gust

3.3 When to Tack

Hopefully most of the time the option when to tack will be your decision, not forced on you by another boat or because you have unintentionally sailed to the layline. Let us go through a few examples.

Before the start you got out on the water nice and early and noticed that the wind which is coming from the North (of a South facing shore) is shifting a lot as the course is not far from the shore line. The range is between 350 and 10 degrees (with 0 being the average). So which tack should you be on?

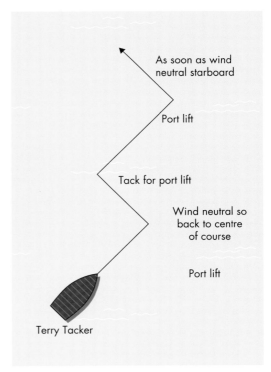

As soon as wind neutral starboard

Port lift

Tack for port lift

Wind neutral so back to centre of course

Port lift

Terry Tacker

3.3a Terry Tacker takes the shifts

Terry Tacker is always on starboard in 10 degrees, port in 350 degrees and on the tack which takes him towards the centre of the race course in 0 degrees.

Now (maybe after several general recalls and not being able to get the race away) the race officer moves the race course 2 miles offshore. Here the wind is between 355 and 5 degrees and a fairly regular oscillation. The key here is to take advantage of the big shift.

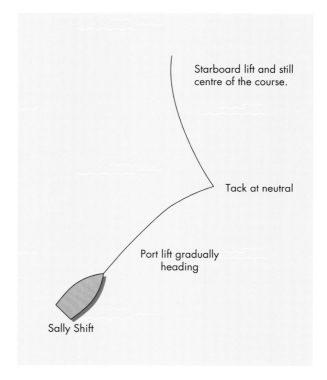

Starboard lift and still centre of the course.

Tack at neutral

Port lift gradually heading

Sally Shift

3.3b Sally Shift sails the wind bend

Sally Shift flips onto starboard as soon as the wind is 0 and increasing and back to port as soon as the wind is 0 degrees to make the most of the big shift.

After the first race which was sailed at low water (to give a large launching area) the tide changes. The direction of the current changes inshore first where the water is shallower.

It is now important to play the current. If the current is across the race course it gives an effective shift meaning it pays to start down current. However be careful that you can cross the line!

If the current is lined up with the wind you need to be heading for the most favourable current or the least adverse current, but be careful with laylines. You don't want to come out of the favourable current too soon and having to do two extra tacks in some boats can be disastrous. Remember the favourable current squeezes the laylines together (making them narrower and it easier to accidently overstand) whereas adverse current stretches the laylines (making them wider and it easier to accidently understand).

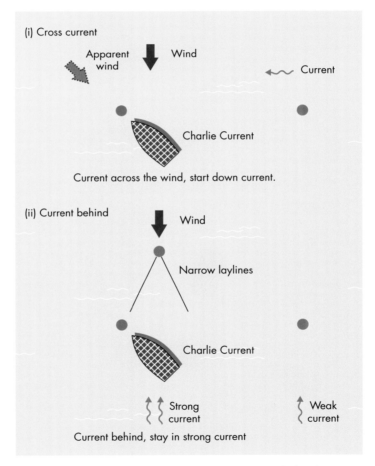

3.3c Charlie Current plays the current: (i) cross current (ii) current behind

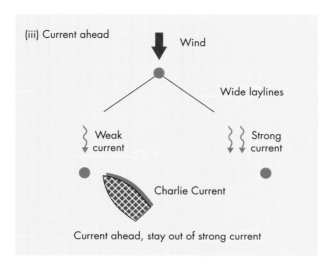

The next day the wind changes direction so that it is now parallel to the land which is quite high, causing a wind bend.

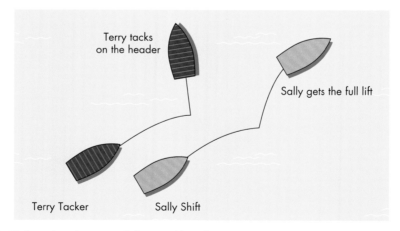

3.3d Sally Shift makes the most of the wind bend

Sally Shift makes the most of this by sailing right into the bend before tacking whereas Terry Tacker loses out by tacking too early.

With the wind dying the course is now brought further inshore but away from the hill. There is now a large difference in pressure (northern hemisphere) with more wind offshore (it would be the opposite in the southern hemisphere).

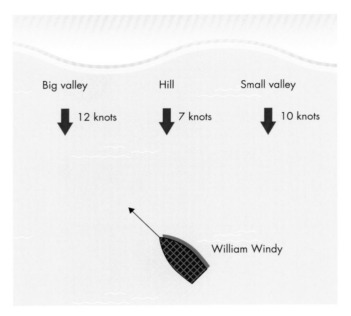

3.3e William Windy is off to get the most wind and win the race

You can easily predict which way the tide will run on the race course by using tidal atlases (these will usually be available from the local chandlery but it may be worth ringing ahead to make sure). However you should always check the current by getting out on the course earlier because predictions are just that, predictions and just like a weather forecast . . . they can be wrong (the predictions are based on past data and do not take account of current conditions such as wind, pressure etc.).

During the course of the day the current is gradually moving to the right and therefore you would expect to gain by going left. Just as you would if the wind was actually going left.

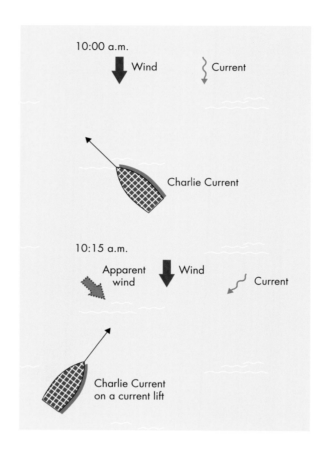

10:00 a.m.

Wind   Current

Charlie Current

10:15 a.m.

Apparent
wind   Wind   Current

Charlie Current
on a current lift

3.3f Charlie Current takes
advantage of the current shift

Note that when allowing for the current, often the effects will be more noticeable on the beat than the run. The best way to tell if you are getting the current correct is to keep taking transits to see where you are going.

Please note when sailing directly with or against the current there is no point pinching or footing unless by doing so it will keep you in less adverse current/get you into less adverse current sooner. As always you should be considering maximum velocity made good (vmg). (The same goes if the current is directly under you.)

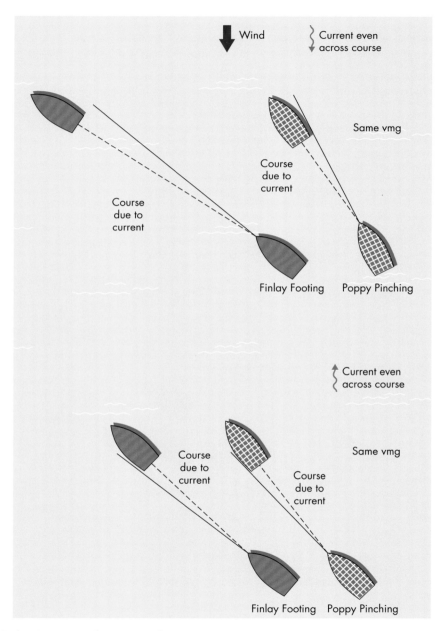

3.3g Finlay Footing and Poppy Pinching

Your final position in relation to the fleet depends on whether you think the wind is going right or left or is constant. Play it safe and try and put yourself in a position so you can take advantage of the next wind shift. So if the wind has shifted to the right you are going left but able to tack as soon as it goes back to the left again.

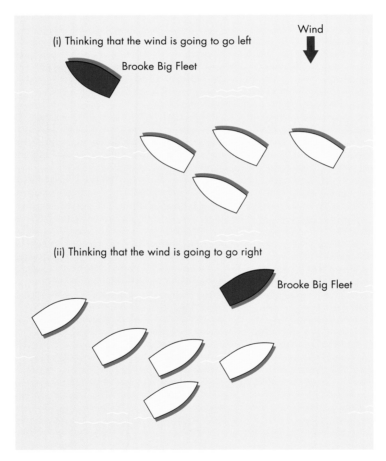

3.3h Brooke Big Fleet playing the fleet (i) expecting left shift (ii) expecting right shift

However you would position yourself further across if you think you know the change is definitely going to happen. For example you know the current is going to change, becoming stronger or weaker or changing direction and therefore affecting the wind (stronger adverse current gives less wind, stronger favourable current gives more wind, cross current gives a wind shift in the downtide direction).

So looking at a cross current left to right, you know the wind is going to shift to the left, or cross current right to left you know the wind is going to shift to the right, so you would position yourself further to the favoured side like Brooke Big Fleet. Or perhaps you can just see what is happening to the fleet in front of you and want to take advantage of this.

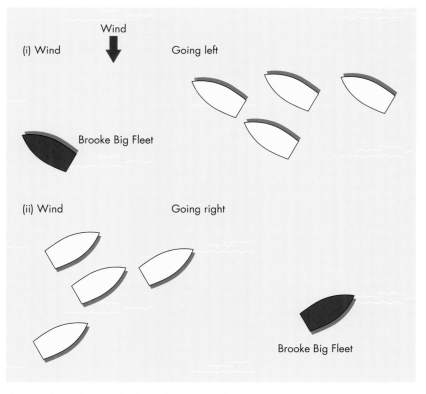

3.3i Brooke Big Fleet playing the fleet, knowing what is going to happen

Chapter 4
The First Beat

First Beat Basics
Meeting Other Boats
Playing it Safe

4.1 First Beat Basics

Your position at the first mark is crucial. After this point it can be hard to make significant place changes. So in a major championship simply being in the top ten round the windward mark can make a real difference to your overall regatta performance. For one thing the front of the fleet tend to fight less amongst themselves and just sail fast, pulling away from everyone else.

With most regattas having many races and few discards, being consistent is very important in order not to get too many high scores. See Chapter 18 Being Consistent.

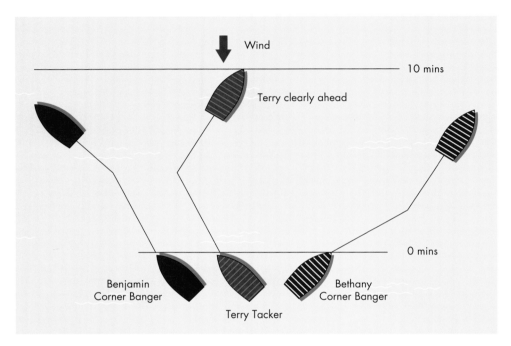

4.1a Terry Tacker tacks on every shift. Everything else being equal this is a safe bet

If you go right to one side of the course then you risk not being able to take advantage of a shift later on (as you are over the laylines) plus you will be sailing extra distance.

To help you stay towards the centre of the course or towards the centre of the favoured side of the course relative to other boats you can alter your mode of sailing. If you are on the left of other boats and you are expecting the wind to go right you want to foot like Finlay to consolidate your gain.

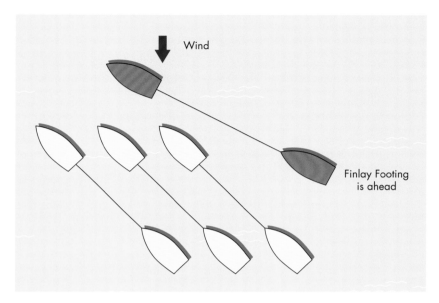

4.1b Finlay Footing consolidates his gain

The class of boat makes a big difference to the way you sail. In a slow boat which turns without losing ground to windward you would tack on the slightest change of a wind shift (perhaps when sailing on a small inland lake surrounded by trees) as there is potential gain to be had for very little loss. However with a faster boat which loses more speed when tacking (a twin trapeze catamaran for example) you would only tack when you are sure it is time to.

4.2   Meeting Other Boats

One of the things about the first beat is that the boats are much closer together and so there tends to be much more boat to boat interaction, meaning the opportunity for place changing is much higher. So you need to make your decision rather than having it forced upon you. Try and think ahead, not only how you are going to get clean wind but how you are going to keep it! The options are as follows:

Maybe you are on port for a reason (you want to get to the right hand side of the course for more pressure or you think a bigger starboard lift is coming). To do a good duck make sure you pass as close to the rudder of the other boat as possible and then head up onto a close hauled course, like Daisy Duck. You may even want to ease the sails and kicker slightly.

Tacking underneath keeps your options open and enables you to carry on sailing in clean wind (to the left), as after all Sophie may be coming across for a reason (starboard may be starting to lift). It also gives Sophie the option to tack back if she wants.

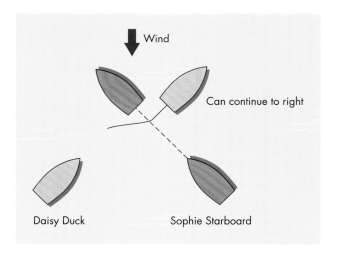

4.2a Carry on and duck with Daisy

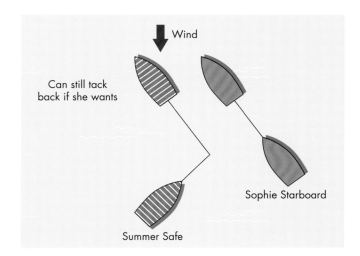

4.2b Tack underneath with Summer Safe

Leebowing is a good option if you want to defend the left hand side of the race track.

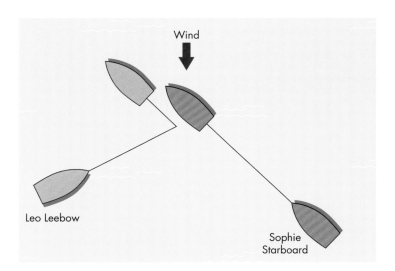

4.2c Leo Leebow leebows Sophie

Leo tacks very close to Sophie (who does not need to alter take avoiding action until Leo is on a close hauled course).

Crossing is obviously the best option but make sure you are well clear or the other boat is going to let you pass.

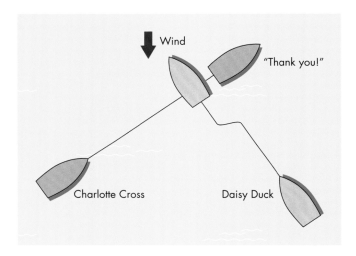

4.2d Daisy Duck lets Charlotte cross

Here Daisy is on starboard, but rather than risking Charlotte tacking and leebowing her she waves her across.

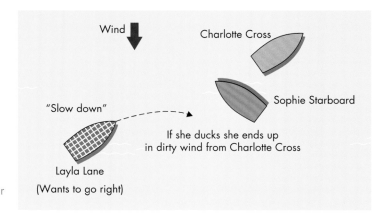

4.2e Layla Lane holds her lane

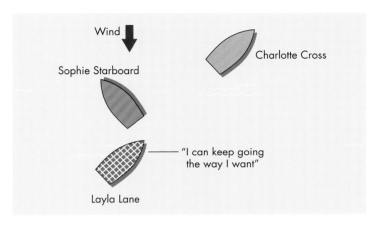

4.2e *(Continued)*

Layla is on port and has a good lane (clean wind in the way she is going). She does not want to tack under Sophie Starboard (because she wants to go to the right) and she does not want to duck or she will be in Charlotte Cross's dirty wind. So she slows down (and loses around half a boat length) before accelerating up to full speed to cross close behind Sophie. She can now continue (with minimum loss) the way she wants to go, still in her lane.

4.3 Playing it Safe

As there are many potential place changes up the first beat (before the start everyone is equal first place) it pays to have a prudent approach. Keep your head out of the boat and see which side of the race track is winning . . . if you are not on that side why not? And can you do something about it? See chapter 19 in *Be Your Own Sailing Coach* as to where you should focus on tactics and where to focus on boatspeed.

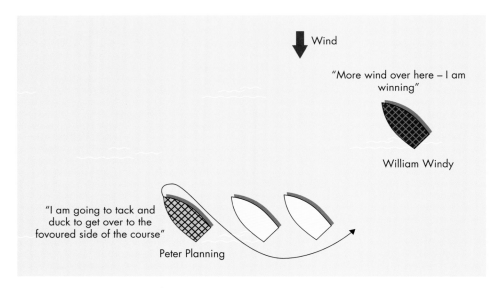

4.3a Peter Planning shows it often pays to take an early loss for a bigger gain later

There is a much higher chance of incidents up the first beat so it pays to stay out of trouble. Remember, when telling someone they can cross, "Go", and "No", can sound very similar! Just shouting back, "Starboard!" or "Keep going", can be much clearer.

However unfortunately incidents do sometimes happen (mainly to Daniel): Daniel Danger is an expert in doing turns. The quickest way to do them in most classes of boat is to bear away and gybe first, as it is much easier to keep your speed up, bear away, gybe and head up than it is to tack, bear away, gybe and head up. Remember, make sure that you have plenty of room to do your turns. You don't want to hit another boat whilst doing them and have to do another set!

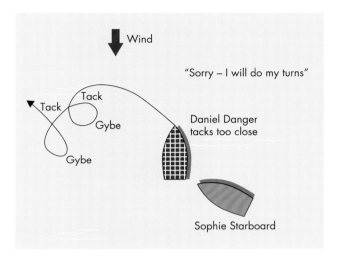

4.3b Daniel Danger doing his turns

However if you cause damage in an incident you have to retire even if you were the right of way boat. So don't hit another boat just to prove a point.

One of the key ideas is to keep your options open. So if the wind becomes shifty or becomes stronger you can take advantage of it or if there is an unexpected change (the wind becomes lighter) you are not vulnerable.

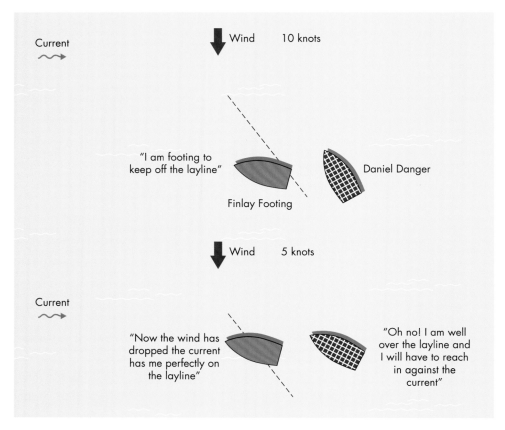

4.3c Finlay Footing is footing to stay off the layline

Chapter 5
Tacking

Basic Tacking

Tacking to Loose Cover

Tacking to Tight Cover

5.1 Basic Tacking

The goal of a good tack is to maximise your gain to windward. This is not the same as completing the tack as quickly as possible (although this may be necessary sometimes) or coming out of the tack as fast as possible. For more details see chapter 6 in *Be Your Own Sailing Coach*. Here Terry Tacker demonstrates three different types of tack:

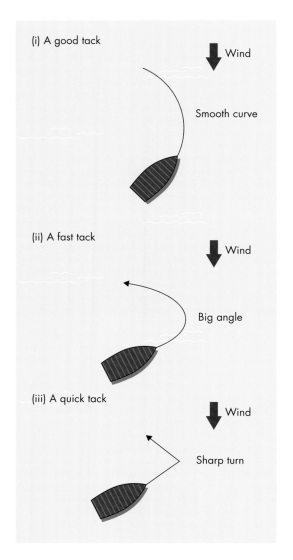

5.1a Terry Tacker demonstrates (i) a good tack (maximising progress to windward) (ii) a fast tack (coming out fast) (iii) a quick tack (tacking as quickly as possible)

You can control your speed of tacking to make sure you end up where you want to be, for example on (not over or under) the layline or on/off another boat by speeding up or slowing down the turn.

When you're just tacking to make it around the course as quickly as possible you always simply want to do a "good" tack. If you then wish to get across to the other side of the race course you would then foot. It is extremely rare that it would pay to do a "crash" tack (where you turn the corner as quickly as possible) as it will take time to get back to full speed and you lose ground to windward.

If you are tacking on a shift (onto the lifting tack) the tack may be quicker than normal as you might only have to tack through 80 degrees (assuming a 10 degree lift). Ideally you tack straight away rather than bearing away then tacking (so as soon as the sail flaps you go). This is why it pays to have your head out of the boat so you know that you can tack as soon as a shift comes in, rather than having to check you can cross etc. Also if there is a slight lift as you tack you may want to slow your tack down as otherwise you may come out slightly below the line you wanted to.

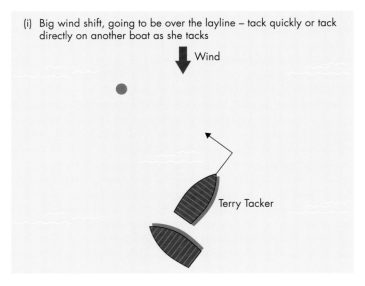

5.1b Terry Tacker controls where he tacks (i) quick tack (ii) slow tack

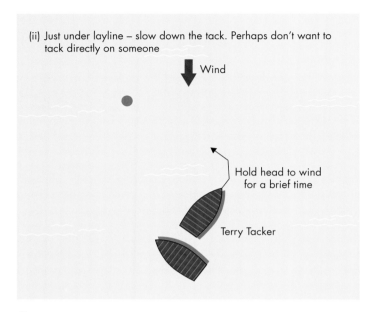

(ii) Just under layline – slow down the tack. Perhaps don't want to tack directly on someone

Wind

Hold head to wind for a brief time

Terry Tacker

5.1b (Continued)

5.2 Tacking to Loose Cover

You may want to stay with a particular boat, for example, if the left hand side of the beat is paying (you are making gains) or you expect it to gain. You don't want to completely separate from the boat or boats but you stick to the side you expect to gain. By not giving them dirty wind they are likely to keep on going.

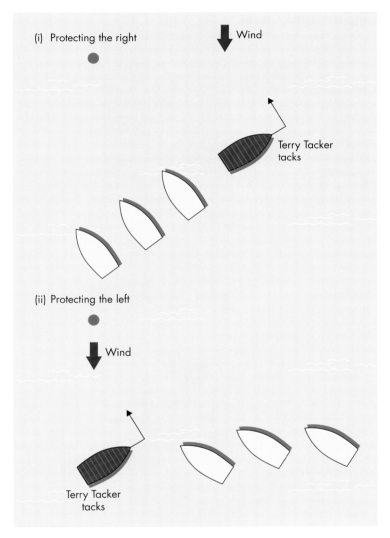

(i) Protecting the right

Wind

Terry Tacker
tacks

(ii) Protecting the left

Wind

Terry Tacker
tacks

5.2a Terry Tacker tacks to give loose cover (i) protecting the right (ii) protecting the left

5.3 Tacking to Tight Cover

Tight cover is applied when you must beat a particular boat (you may even need to sail that boat down the fleet) and are not worried about other boats overtaking you both. Here you are positioned directly to windward, giving far more dirty wind. You need to watch them closely to tack as they tack but being wary of dummy tacks! You may find you end up both slowing each other down, especially in boats which lose lots of ground to windward when tacking.

Tight cover can be a way of "shepherding" a boat or boats. For example if you want the fleet to go right you can tight cover on starboard and loose cover on port. This will make them want to go on port (to the right) because this is the only way they have clean air. To tack in precisely the right place you may need to speed up or slow your tack down.

5.3a Terry Tacker tight covers on starboard

Chapter 6
Windward Mark

Laylines
Other Boats
Starboard Roundings

6.1   Laylines

An early layline call makes you vulnerable to a wind shift. So if you are sailing to the corners, perhaps to clear your wind after a bad start, try and avoid the laylines as if you get on them too early and there is a shift then you lose out by either overstanding the mark or having to sail extra distance. Here we can see how Terry Tacker has the advantage over Benjamin and Bethany Corner Bangers.

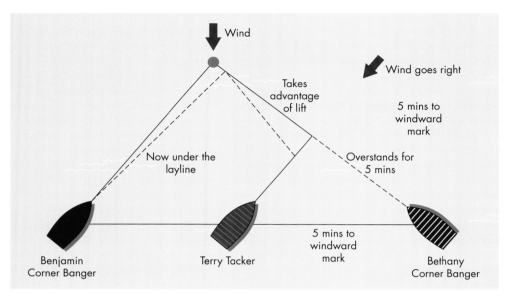

Wind

Wind goes right

Takes advantage of lift

5 mins to windward mark

Now under the layline

Overstands for 5 mins

Benjamin Corner Banger

Terry Tacker

5 mins to windward mark

Bethany Corner Banger

or

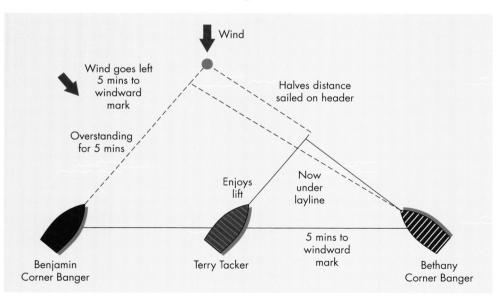

Wind

Wind goes left 5 mins to windward mark

Halves distance sailed on header

Overstanding for 5 mins

Enjoys lift

Now under layline

Benjamin Corner Banger

Terry Tacker

5 mins to windward mark

Bethany Corner Banger

6.1a Laylines with Terry Tacker, Benjamin and Bethany Corner Bangers

It is worth noting that if there were more shifts to the right than the left then you would want to sail back to the centre of the course when the wind was in its average direction.

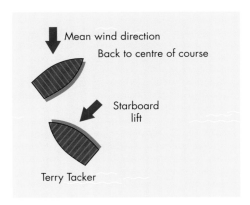

Mean wind direction

Back to centre of course

Starboard lift

Terry Tacker

6.1b Terry Tacker staying in the centre of the course

When you get close to the laylines there are lots of places to be won and lost just like any other part of the course where boats come close together. See Chapter 4.2.

6.2 Other Boats

Getting on the layline early (giving you a "long layline") will rarely pay but when you get on the layline you want to ensure that you get it right and in a perfect world other boats get it wrong! If the course is offset (you spend more time on one tack than the other) then you want to do the "long" tack first (the one which you are going to spend more time on) as this will keep you further from the laylines.

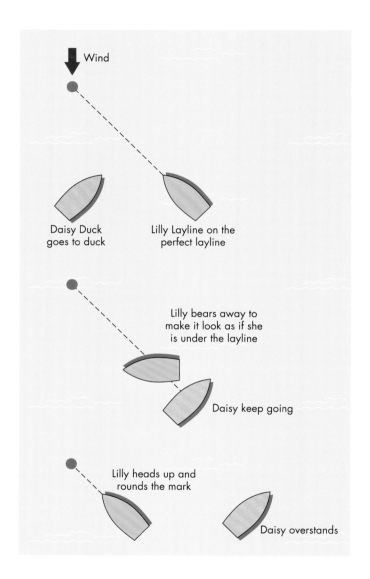

Wind

Daisy Duck
goes to duck

Lilly Layline on the
perfect layline

Lilly bears away to
make it look as if she
is under the layline

Daisy keep going

Lilly heads up and
rounds the mark

Daisy overstands

6.2a Lilly Layline makes
Daisy Duck overstand the
windward mark

Here Lilly Layline, who is an expert on laylines, bears away as Daisy ducks behind her making Daisy think that she has further to sail to the layline than she does. She then heads back up having gained significantly on Daisy.

Lilly can also force Daniel Danger into a very dangerous position, underneath the layline and unable to tack, by sailing a bit lower and faster and once again heading up as the "other boat" tacks. Here Daniel is in big trouble and will most likely have to gybe round and look for a gap in the line of boats on the starboard layline.

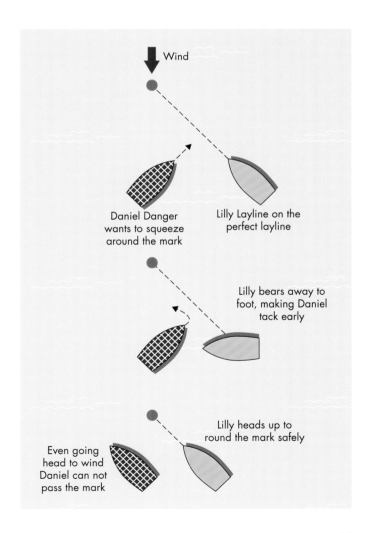

Wind

Daniel Danger wants to squeeze around the mark

Lilly Layline on the perfect layline

Lilly bears away to foot, making Daniel tack early

Lilly heads up to round the mark safely

Even going head to wind Daniel can not pass the mark

6.2b Lilly Layline makes Daniel Danger understand the windward mark

Poor old Daniel is not having a lovely time. He once again tries to get around the windward mark (whilst Lilly is sailing into the distance) and he tacks inside three boat lengths. The boats who are on the layline have to luff up above close hauled and quite rightly protest Daniel.

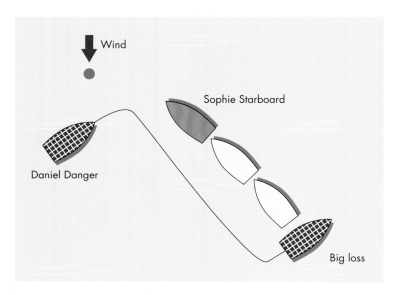

6.2c Daniel Danger tacks inside three boat lengths

What he should have done is carry on and then tack above the layline without infringing anyone like Sarah Safe. Remember a lot of boats will play it slightly safe and overstand the layline a bit so if you hit the layline too early you may well end up overstanding a great deal . . . You have infringed a boat if they head up past close hauled. If they were reaching and headed up to close hauled course then you have not infringed.

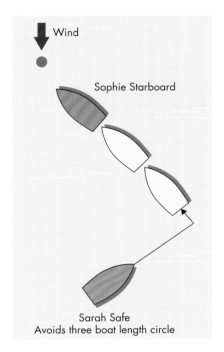

6.2d Sarah Safe crosses behind the line of boats and tacks above the layline

Finally, remember when choosing your layline that you can if necessary pinch up to (but not beyond) head to wind to shoot the mark. This is a very useful skill to have in the tool box.

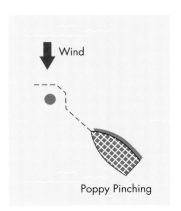

6.2e Poppy Pinching shoots head to wind around the mark

65

6.3   Starboard Roundings

Rare but certainly not unheard of is rounding the windward mark to starboard. This is probably one of the reasons there is often confusion with the rules. *The Rules in Practice* by Bryan Willis is a highly recommended read and just like this book should always be in your regatta kit bag!

Just like any other windward mark you can rarely approach on starboard unless you are well clear of other boats like Tilley Traffic.

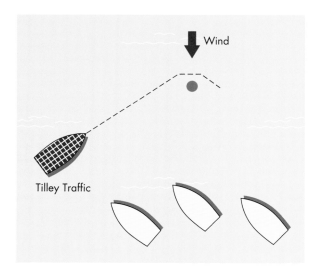

Wind

Tilley Traffic

6.3a Tilley Traffic approaches with speed on the port layline (making it for an easy spinnaker hoist for the downwind leg)

So the safest option is to approach on the starboard layline like Sophie Starboard. Here you need to be careful that you do not duck like Daniel Danger and end up the wrong side of the mark. Remember if you are on the layline and duck a boat then you are no longer on the layline.

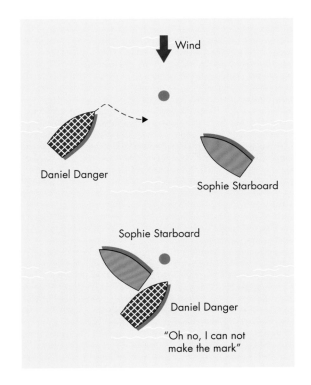

6.3b Daniel Danger gets caught out by Sophie Starboard

Better to have a plan like Peter Planning either to tack (and tack back as soon as possible) or just to slow down but hold your course.

If there is a lot of traffic and you have no choice but to come in from the left hand side of the course then avoiding the other boats like Tilley Traffic is probably your best option. This way you lose a couple of boat lengths early on but avoid the mess at the mark.

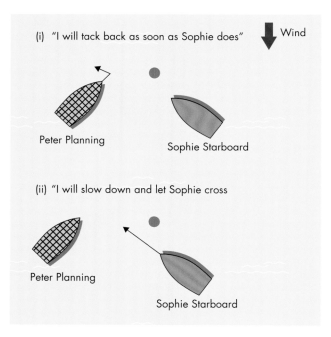

6.3c Peter Planning has two options: (i) to tack and then tack back as soon as Sophie does or (ii) to slow down and let Sophie cross

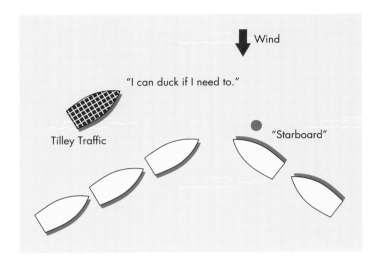

6.3d Tilley Traffic above the port layline for safety

It is very important that you keep concentrating after the windward mark, after all you are on port when many of the fleet who are approaching the windward mark may be on starboard and some may have overstood the layline. You want to make sure you have a clean lane going downwind.

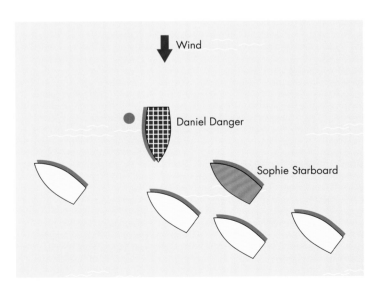

6.3e Daniel Danger is in the danger zone

Chapter 7
Tight Reaching

Tight Reaching Basics
Dealing with the Conditions
Dealing with Other Boats

7.1 Tight Reaching Basics

One of the most important decisions to make is whether to hoist the kite and if so when! If you get it wrong and hoist too early then you can make a big loss. Get it right and expect to make a significant gain on the fleet as there can be a large speed advantage to be flying the kite when other boats are not. For more details on rig set see chapter 12 in *Be Your Own Sailing Coach*.

You must also consider current very carefully as when your angle changes so does the effect on the current. Once again the danger is ending up too low for the mark. This may mean you have to drop the kite to make it up and beat back up to the mark or worse still end up putting in a tack on a reach leg.

Many regattas will have a spacer mark before the downwind leg. This means you have a short tight reach to separate the fleet and avoid the carnage at the windward mark with boats going downwind meeting those going back upwind. This is especially important for large fleets (perhaps sailing a sausage or inner loop) or very fast boats like twin trapeze catamarans. It is therefore important that the rig is set for a tight reach then adjusted when you go round the second mark for the run (not set for the run as soon as you round the windward mark).

7.2 Dealing with the Conditions

Important information is what is the wind doing? Was it lifting at the windward mark? And if so do you think it will continue to lift? Or is it now going to start to head? Are you expecting the wind to increase or decrease along the leg?

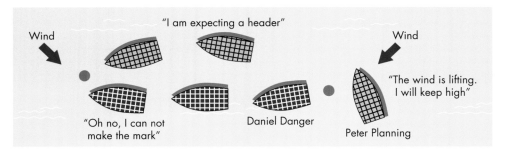

7.2a Peter Planning expects the wind shift

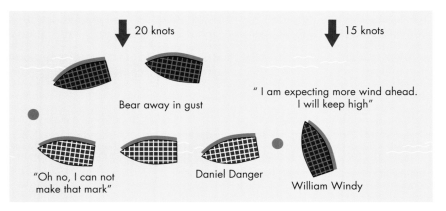

7.2b William Windy expects more wind ahead

7.3   Dealing with Other Boats

Being rolled to windward on a tight reach is death. Not only will one boat go over you but probably several as you get slowed down by all the dirty wind and because of the tightness of the leg you probably can not bear away to clean your wind. Even if the mark is a port rounding (so you would have room at the mark) you would think very hard about going low if it would put you in someone's dirty wind.

7.3a Daniel Danger gets himself in a spot of bother

Chapter 8
Beam Reaching

Beam Reaching Basics
Dealing with the Conditions
Dealing with Other Boats

In a steadier wind the key thing is to minimise the distance sailed to the mark. However you must allow for the current especially if the wind is light compared to the strength of the current. If you simply point at the mark you will sail a lot of extra distance as shown here by Sid Straight Line and Archie Arc.

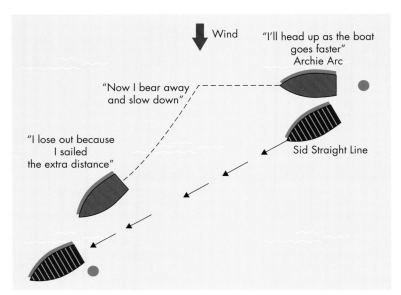

8.1a Sid Straight Line and Archie Arc no current

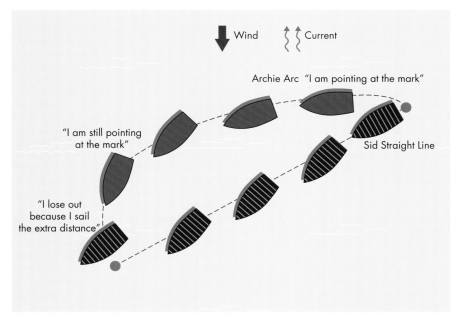

8.1b Sid Straight Line and Archie Arc in current

8.2 Dealing with the Conditions

In medium winds where there are gusts you wish to stay in the gusts as long as possible to keep your average speed up. So you would bear away in the gusts and then afterwards head back up in the lulls. In planing conditions you would often want to bear away as far as possible without coming off the plane before coming back up as high as required to stay on the plane. If you spend the whole leg planing when other people are on and off the plane you will be amongst the quickest in the fleet.

In strong winds to avoid a broach bear away hard as the gust hits so as to take full advantage of it but also to depower it. You can then head back up after the gust passes. If you are struggling to get back to the mark make sure you hike/trapeze as hard as possible and if necessary allow the sails to flap somewhat rather than having the boat heel excessively.

Here if you followed Georgia Gust closely on a gusty day you would see her making large movements up and downwind but viewed from a long way above it would look more like a straight line.

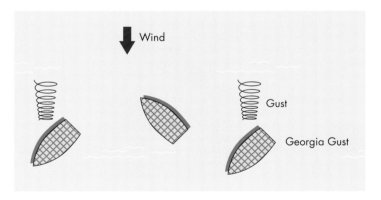

8.2a Down in the gusts and up in the lulls with Georgia Gust seeing pressure on the water

For more details on speed see chapter 12 in *Be Your Own Sailing Coach.*

8.3 Dealing with Other Boats

On the beam reach you have the greatest range of course. On a gusty day you could be sailing on anything from a tight reach to a beam reach. The problem is that the fleet tends to act like a flock of sheep – all following each other. You can take advantage of this by keeping away from the fleet.

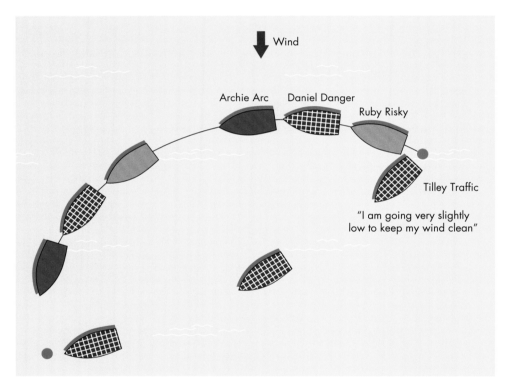

8.3a Tilley Traffic overtakes the pack ahead

Chapter 9
Broad Reaching

Broad Reaching Basics
Dealing with the Conditions
Dealing with Other Boats

9.1   Broad Reaching Basics

Don't be tempted to relax on this leg of the course (just because physically it may be easier than beating or sailing a tighter reach). Just like on any other leg you need to know whether to prioritise shifts or pressure, but on a broad reach it is often pressure.

You are unlikely to be overpowered on a broad reach unless it is survival conditions. More often the problem is that you end up high of the mark after you have headed up to increase your speed and you are then unable to bear away back down to the mark without a huge drop in speed.

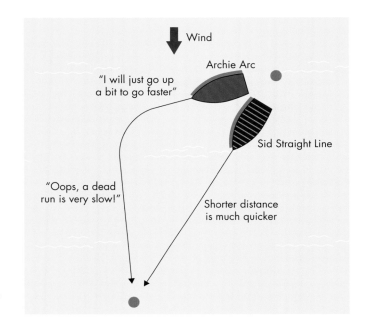

9.1a Archie Arc sailing a big curve downwind compared to Sid Straight Line

You can of course see the wind or rather its effect on the water, and indeed on other boats, so you should be able to see what is happening.

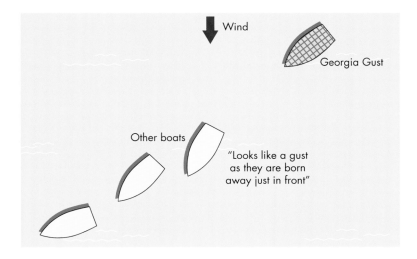

9.1b Georgia Gust looking at other boats on the water

You also need to take a view as to the time frame. Is it worth going up or down for a gust/lull which you can see on the water but which might never come? Going up will get you into the gust sooner and once in a gust bearing away will keep you in it longer.

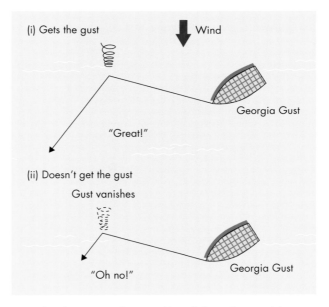

9.1c Georgia Gust goes for the gust and gets it (i) and doesn't get it (ii)

Inland you may expect to steer a lot to maximise the time spent in the gust and to react to change in wind direction. However the faster the boat the less steering you would tend to do in relation to the change. Too much steering could slow you down in a boat which is already planing as opposed to one which has not yet reached full displacement speed.

Even when it is very windy you still need to think about your racing tactics. You should not simply be hanging on and enjoying the ride (or simply surviving), you should be trying to get round the course as quickly as possible!

For more details on soaking low see chapter 12 in *Be Your Own Sailing Coach*.

9.2 Dealing with the Conditions

It is important to notice if any changes are continuous, for example is the current gradually increasing or changing direction? This may mean you need to position yourself where there is more favourable current or where you expect there to be more favourable current soon. For example if you round the windward mark in slack current you might expect the current to change inshore first so you would position yourself to take advantage of this (if the benefit of the current is greater than the cost of sailing the extra distance).

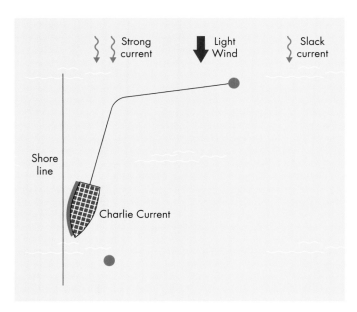

9.2a Charlie Current makes the most of the favourable current

9.3 Dealing with Other Boats

Unlike a run you can not simply gybe off to clean your wind (as the extra distance sailed is unlikely to be made up). So defending is harder. Therefore you need to make it clear to boats behind that you are not going to let them roll over the top of you.

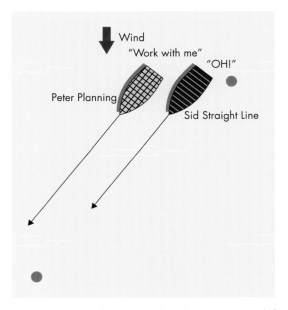

9.3a Peter Planning goes up slightly and makes it clear he is going to defend his position

Chapter 10
Running Symmetric

Basic Running

Downwind in Waves

Sailing Aggressively

10.1 Basic Running

Getting the angle downwind is very important and as conditions change the fast angle to sail downwind will change also (a good example of a transition would be from non-planing to planing conditions).

When sailing low like Lucas you need to be very careful that the spinnaker does not collapse, as you would then need to head up a lot to refill the spinnaker.

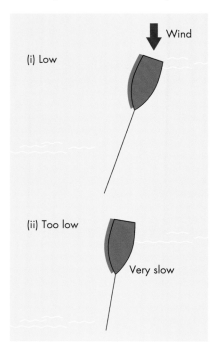

10.1a Lucas Low sailing (i) low and (ii) too low

In a single hander with an unstayed rig like a Laser you can sail very effectively by the lee like Lewis Lee. Here the flow of wind goes from the leech to the luff (the mast is now acting as the leech and due to its stiffness the flow is very stable). It also gives you good tactical options allowing you to move around to keep your wind clean and gives you better options to stay surfing on a wave or in pressure without having to put in a gybe.

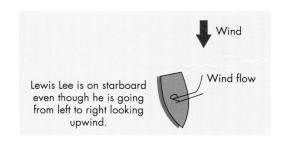

10.1b Looking upwind Lewis Lee demonstrating sailing by the lee

You need to be very careful downwind to keep your wind clear or potentially you could lose a lot of places as once you get rolled you are more vulnerable to it happening again. Get your head out of the boat and make sure you have a clear lane to sail in, just like you would upwind. Pressure is often the most important thing downwind.

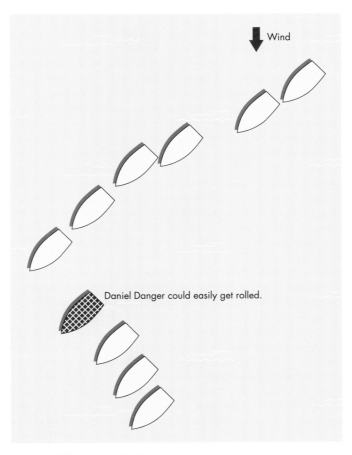

10.1c Daniel Danger could be in trouble!

The aim is to link the pressure like William Windy but also to try and stay in the shifts as well. Although these happen less frequently downwind, in a boat with an unstayed rig you would not have to gybe to stay in the shifts but alternate between broad reaching and sailing by the lee. In a stayed boat you would gybe to stay on the heading tack. You should have an idea of the angles (and also where the pressure is) from the beat.

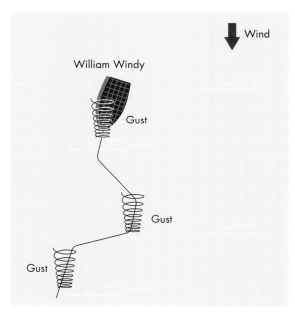

10.1d William Windy stays in the pressure downwind

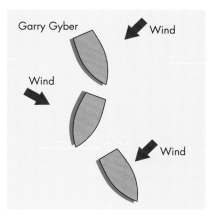

10.1e Garry Gyber gybes to stay on the heading tack

You should also know from the beat where the course is square and if not (due to the placement of the buoys or the current) you should keep your options open by sailing the long tack first. You should of course always try and avoid as much adverse current as possible and take advantage of any favourable current.

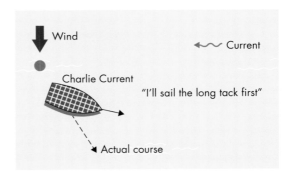

10.1f Charlie Current sails the long tack first

10.2 Downwind in Waves

However it is not only the wind you need to address. There are also waves. There are basically three transitional stages (as opposed to planing where you either are or you aren't).

Not surfing – keep as low as you can without losing speed. In many classes this will be very nearly dead downwind.

(i) Marginal surfing – head up or sail by the lee to catch waves.

(ii) Consistent surfing – you can now pass waves. Just aim for the flat spots as you overtake the waves!

The course may be offset. That is you may spend more time on one tack downwind than the other. This may be due to the wind angle or it may be due to the waves. If it is due to the wind angle then you sail the long tack first just like upwind. However if it is due to waves sail the fast tack first. This will allow you to extend and get cleaner wind. If you can surf, surf. There is no guarantee those waves will be there later!

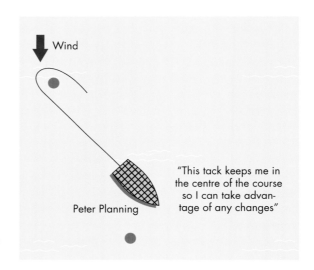

10.2a Peter Planning sails the long downwind tack first

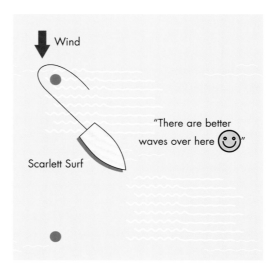

10.2b Scarlett Surf making the best of the waves downwind

In very light winds where you can not surf properly the course may become offset where the waves push you one way, rather like current (but don't actually give you a speed advantage because you can not surf). Here you would sail the longest tack first.

10.3   Sailing Aggressively

It is still possible to gain places downwind by controlling the other boats, if you are in a position to stop them gybing until the time you wish. You turn parallel to the other boat, completely covering it and making it very hard for it to set the spinnaker. You need to plan your attack perfectly so everyone knows what they are doing (gybing, soaking or going high) and are prepared, but if at all possible don't give any signs about what you are planning, so the other boats can prepare or change their plans!

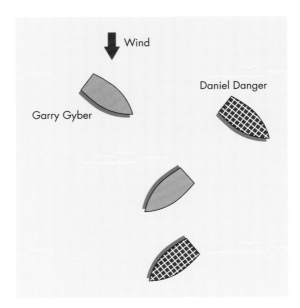

10.3a Garry Gyber gybes right onto the wind of Daniel Danger

Then to close the gap Garry stays directly upwind to give maximum wind shadow. As Daniel slows down, Garry then soaks low to close the gap.

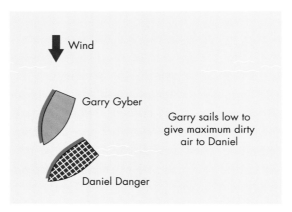

Wind

Garry Gyber

Garry sails low to give maximum dirty air to Daniel

Daniel Danger

10.3b Garry Gyber in control of Daniel Danger

Chapter 11
Running Asymmetric

Basic Running

Gybe Set

Sailing Aggressively

11.1 Basic Running

The key difference between a traditional run and an asymmetric run is the apparent wind where due to the boat travelling faster the wind appears to come from further forward than the true wind. This means differences in boatspeed are significant (gusts become very important as the faster we go, the faster we sail through them) as is sailing. Having said this trapeze boats with large symmetrical kites can travel very fast downwind and are therefore influenced by apparent wind. For more information see chapter 13 in *Be Your Own Sailing Coach*.

Hitting the right angle downwind is very important in an asymmetric. Go too low like Lucas Low and it is easy to get rolled. Go too high like Harry High and it is easy to get pinned out so you can not gybe.

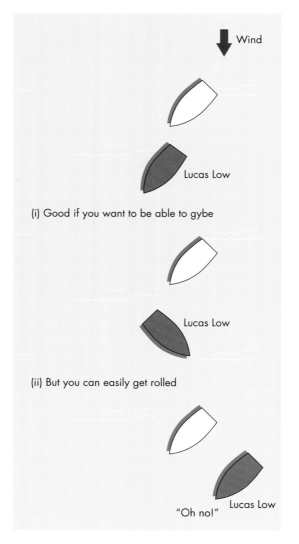

11.1a Lucas Low (i) good if you want to be able to gybe (ii) but you can easily get rolled

11.1b Harry High (i) good if wind is heading or you are sailing into more pressure (ii) bad if you want to gybe

In strong winds the answer is usually easy – get your weight out as much as possible (through hard hiking/trapezing) and the boat will readily come up to top speed, bringing on plenty of apparent wind enabling you to go lower. You may even end up going faster and lower than boats which are trying to go low.

When sailing on apparent wind you need to look ahead to see what the breeze is going to be doing. The further ahead you can look (and therefore plan) the better.

11.2   Gybe Set

The Gybe set is a good option if you wish to protect the right hand side of the course (maybe there is more wind/better current or the wind is moving right), especially if the leg is quite short.

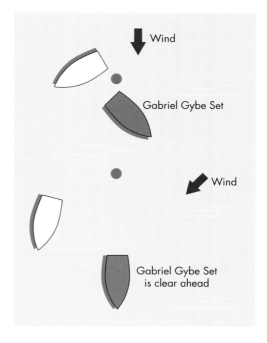

11.2a Gabriel Gybe Set wind moving right

You must make sure you are prepared to do this as turning the boat through 180 degrees is a much more difficult manoeuvre than a simple bear away and hoist. The key thing is to keep the speed up and make the turn as smooth as possible. Do not come in on port tack (as this would make it a 270 degree turn) unless you have no choice. Even if you can tack and sail for one boat length (to get some speed back up) it is much better than trying to do a tack and a gybe around the mark. Be aware of those people sailing upwind (on starboard) on the starboard layline.

11.3   Sailing Aggressively

You want to take each gust down but you need to be careful of boats going high which could roll you .You want your focus to be on steering accurately for the wind and the waves. You don't want to have all your attention on one boat when you are racing against a whole fleet! So either go high or gybe off, unless you are comfortably clear of the boats behind.

Remember a good mark rounding (exiting at full speed with the kite pulling as soon as possible) will make your life much easier. Depending on what you want you can go up high and make it clear you are not going to let yourself be rolled, or you can gybe off. Don't get in the danger zone like Daniel Danger.

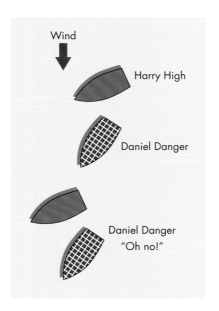

11.3a Daniel Danger is in danger of being rolled by Harry High

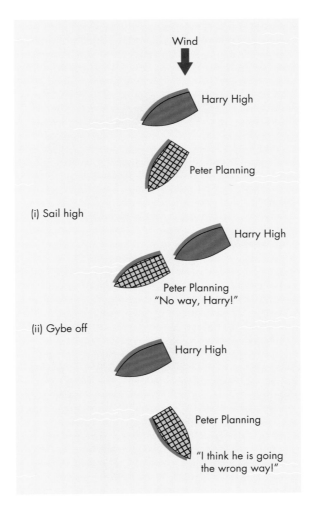

11.3b Peter Planning has two plans to do a deal with Harry High (i) sail high or (ii) gybe off

To guarantee you have gained a place you can simply sail the other boat on until you hit the layline much like you would upwind. Also remember the angle of dirty wind is further forward due to the apparent wind so consider this when you choose where to gybe. Gybing usually slows the boat down considerably. It is often better to slow down and go behind a right of way boat and then to gybe off.

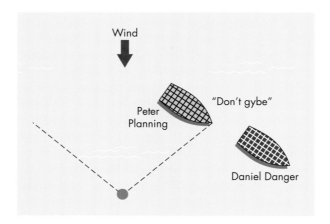

11.3c Daniel Danger gets sailed off

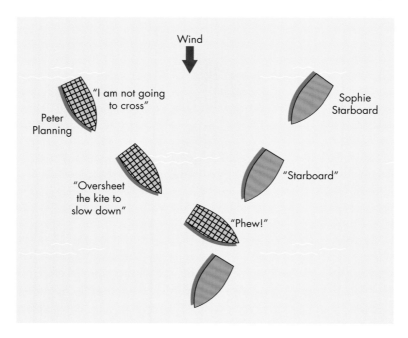

11.3d Peter Planning slows down to get down the run faster!

Chapter 12
Gybing

At the Gybe Mark

The Manoeuvre Itself

The Angle

12.1   At the Gybe Mark

The best way to get room on a boat is to work your way high then come lower on the final section of the leg. The way to defend against this is to sail (fast) in a straight line to the mark allowing for any current.

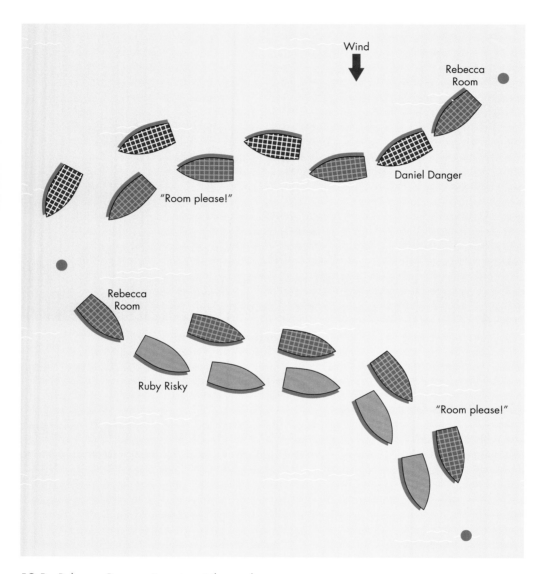

12.1a Rebecca Room gets water at the mark

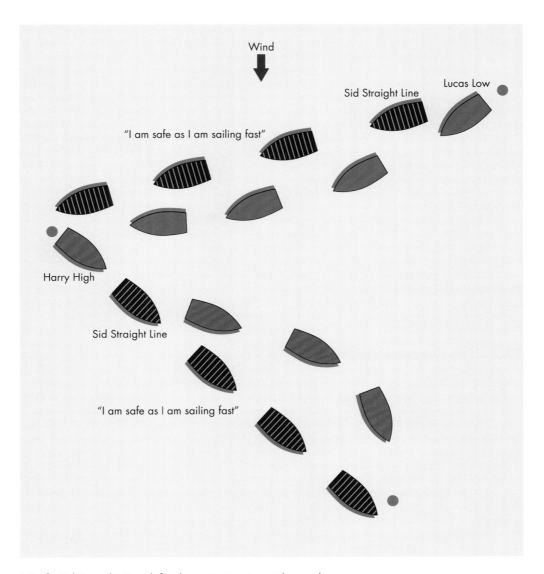

Wind

Sid Straight Line

Lucas Low

"I am safe as I am sailing fast"

Harry High

Sid Straight Line

"I am safe as I am sailing fast"

12.1b Sid Straight Line defends against water at the mark

When you gybe you need to consider the next leg of the course. So you exit the gybe on the new angle for the next leg.

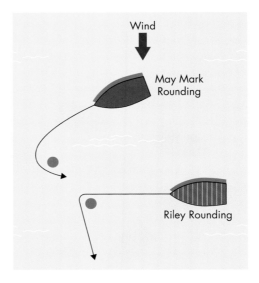

12.1c May Mark Rounding goes from a beam reach to a beam reach. Whilst Riley Rounding goes from a tight reach to a broad reach

12.2 The Manoeuvre Itself

Speed into the gybe really helps with speed out. This is why tactically having room to turn is crucial. You are much less likely to have problems when the rig is light than when it is really loaded up (so gybe in the gust when you are at full speed not just before the gust hits you!). As long as you get these "big" things right then you can correct any "little" mistakes you make (sheeting, steering or bodyweight errors) fairly easily.

- Always turn using a smooth curve, starting when surfing down a wave or in short chop in a "flat" bit.
- Move your bodyweight as the boat heels to windward and turns so you are on the new windward side as the sails fill. The rudder should be centred (so the rudder and centreboard are in line and not acting as a brake) to accelerate the boat away.

For more details see chapter 6 in *Be Your Own Sailing Coach*.

12.3 The Angle

The faster your boat the bigger the angle you turn through when you gybe on a dead downwind leg. In other words if you are sailing mainly on apparent wind then you will perhaps go through 90 degrees when you gybe (a similar angle to tacking) but if you are in true wind you will wish to avoid altering course as much as possible, as you would simply be sailing extra distance. The windier it is the smaller the angle you turn through when run to run gybing as you will be sailing lower.

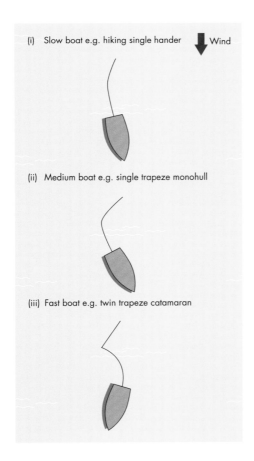

(i) Slow boat e.g. hiking single hander   Wind

(ii) Medium boat e.g. single trapeze monohull

(iii) Fast boat e.g. twin trapeze catamaran

12.3a Gybing the best angle with Garry Gybe: (i) Slow boat e.g. hiking single hander (ii) Medium boat e.g. single trapeze monohull (iii) Fast boat e.g. twin trapeze catamaran

Chapter 13
Leeward Mark

Basic Leeward Mark Rounding

Leeward Mark Rounding with Other Boats

Giving or Taking Room at the Leeward Mark

13.1 Basic Leeward Mark Rounding

A good leeward mark rounding is essential to set yourself up for the next beat. The golden rule is in wide and out tight. This means you can tack when you want, or if you wish to keep going then you can do so in clean air. The aim is to pass the mark at full speed on a close hauled course so if you took a picture and edited it to remove the mark you could not tell the boat had just rounded a mark.

The amount of space required obviously depends upon the wind strength and waves (the windier and wavier it is the more space you need to do a good rounding) and different classes of boat will perform differently. However a smooth rounding, using minimum rudder, will work well in most boats as a sharp turn tends to bleed speed.

Remember practice make permanent. On your own, practise rounding a leeward mark until the drill becomes second nature and you no longer have to think about it, leaving you free to get your head out of the boat to consider your tactical options for the next beat. In boats with a spinnaker timing is even more important, as it can be very slow trying to sail upwind with the spinnaker!

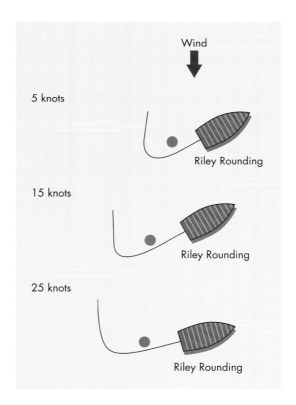

13.1a Riley Rounding

13.2 Leeward Mark Rounding with Other Boats

In the absence of other boats you will approach the mark at full pace – as if you were doing a time trial around the race course. However the presence of other boats around you may limit your options.

If you do a poor rounding like Samuel Sloppy you have no clear lane and the only way to get clean wind would be to tack off. This is especially damaging in light winds.

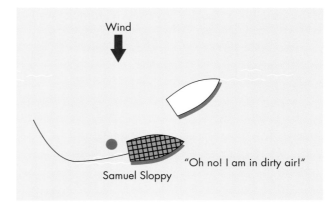

13.2a Samuel Sloppy does a poor mark rounding

If you wish to tack off or the boat in front has sailed high around the mark then you may need to pinch up (sail close to the wind) in order to ensure you can tack/keep your wind clean.

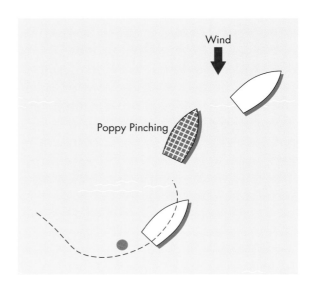

13.2b Poppy Pinching can tack off if she wants

The racing line would be a line you would take in the absence of other boats (if you were doing a time trial or a handicap race with no other boats close to you).

You must of course allow for the current. Charlie Current would be the outside boat at the mark but in fact he has allowed for the current perfectly.

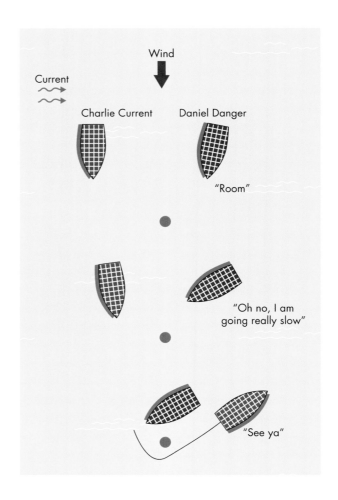

13.2c Charlie Current stitches up Daniel Danger

Before you get to the mark you should have considered your plan for the next beat so you can execute it easily. Here Peter Planning knows he wants to go left and he has several options as to when to tack. He will go at his earliest opportunity but will wait for a lane if other boats tack first. If he simply needed to sail on then a good rounding and good speed would be enough.

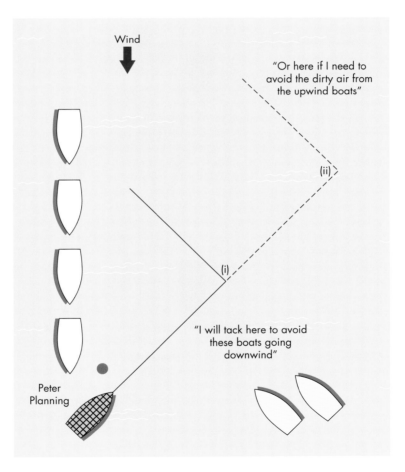

13.2d Peter Planning knows what he wants to do

Remember sometimes the best mark rounding may be achieved by slowing down. It rarely pays to sail around a group of boats. The better option is usually to slow down to ensure a good mark rounding. This can be achieved through rapid steering head up, bearing away, heading up, bearing away etc. to sail distance.

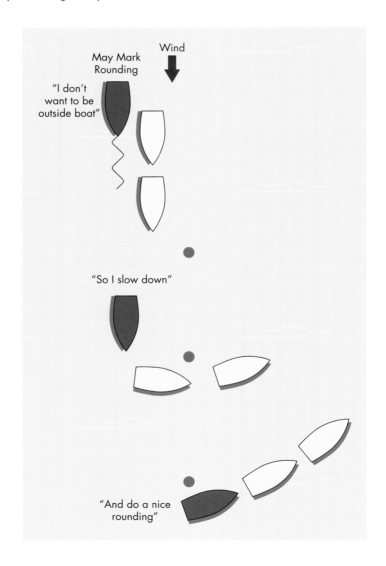

13.2e May Mark Rounding's patience is rewarded

13.3 Giving or Taking Room at the Leeward Mark

Remember at a leeward mark you are entitled to room to make a seaman like rounding, that is the minimum amount of room required to go around the mark. If you take enough room for a racing rounding you could end up in the protest room. Likewise you should not allow someone to take more room than is required.

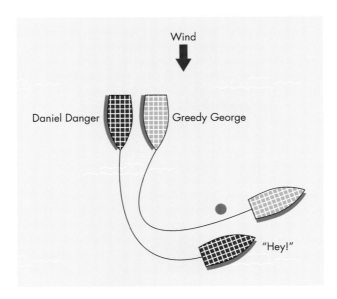

13.3a George Greedy takes too much room

The amount of space required means that actually the boat giving room is in control and therefore should also be able to make a good mark rounding.

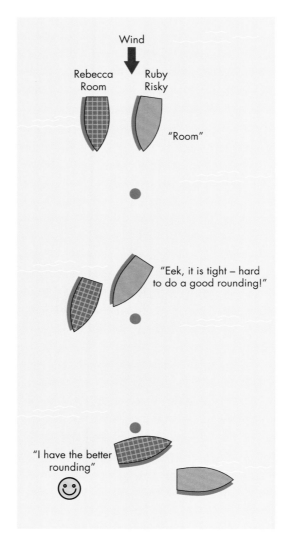

13.3b Rebecca Room and Ruby Risky go round the leeward mark together

Of course if there is the option of not having to give room this is often preferable. (Although you wouldn't want to lose lots of ground downwind just to stop one boat rounding inside you or risk trying to break the overlap and failing.)

Here thinking ahead really counts. Maybe 80% of the downwind leg is about speed but near the marks you need to be making decisions, not having decisions made for you.

By luffing (heading up) then bearing away just before the give room zone you can break the overlap as does Oliver Overlap. The current give room zone is three hull lengths (this does not include rudder, spinnaker pole etc.) although class rules or sailing instructions could change this.

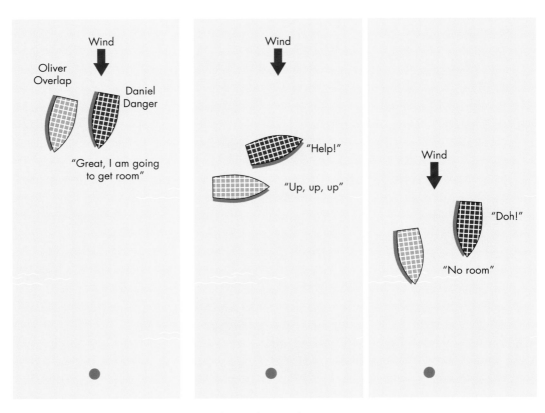

13.3c Oliver Overlap breaks his overlap with Daniel Danger

However a right of way boat as opposed to one who is simply entitled to room can make a racing rounding. So when Riley is on starboard she can keep sailing to the point of a racing rounding before gybing and she must be given enough room to gybe (remember the boom has to come across!!!).

13.3d Riley Rounding comes in on starboard

Chapter 14
Leeward Gates

Choosing Which Gate to Round

Rounding with Other Boats

Sailing Aggressively

14.1 Choosing Which Gate to Round

Due to the extremely tight nature of modern racing it is often necessary to have a leeward gate rather than a single mark to avoid the carnage that would result in everyone trying to go round the same mark. This is especially true of modern asymmetric boats which plane downwind.

Just like a start line or finish line there will usually be a bias to the gate as with changing wind and current it is extremely hard to set the marks absolutely square to the wind. The further apart these marks are the more important this is.

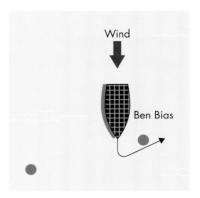

14.1a Ben Bias chooses the closest gate

However you may choose your gate on the basis of which way you want to go up the next beat, especially in a boat which loses lots of speed when tacking.

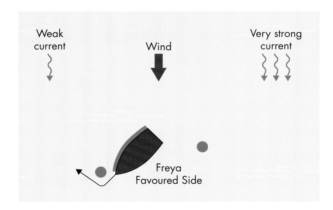

14.1b Freya Favoured Side chooses to get over to the favoured side of the beat asap

Or it may be a case of trying to do a good rounding and therefore choosing the gate which has the least traffic around it. Not only will it make it easier for you to do a good mark rounding (without having to slow down if you don't have room or are having to defend your position) but it is likely to give you more options up the next beat.

Your approach will of course depend upon the proximity of other boats. When going round the starboard gate with other boats for example you may choose to come

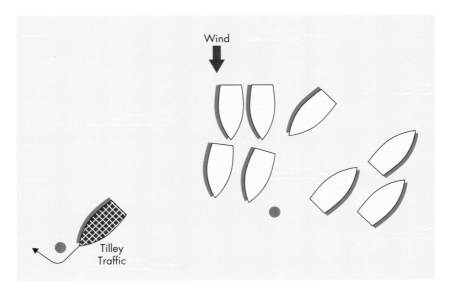

14.1c Tilley Traffic keeping away from the pack of boats

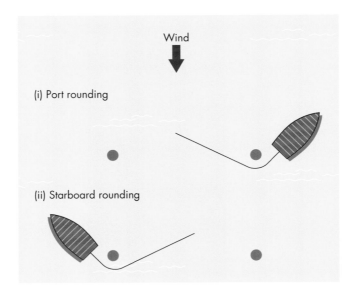

14.1d Riley Rounding doing a (i) port and (ii) starboard rounding in the absence of other boats

from the right so you are coming in as the inside boat on starboard. However if you are well clear of the boats behind, you may choose to come on port to make it easier to do a good mark rounding.

If you are going for the port gate then if you are well clear you could simply come in on starboard but if boats are close to you not only do you risk having to give room at the mark but you could be sailing through a large area of dirty air. It's better to come in from the left but remember since you are on port you are the give way boat until the three boat lengths circle.

14.2   Rounding with Other Boats

Sailing the shortest distance and being the inside boat at the favoured gate is vital and can save sailing a lot of extra distance.

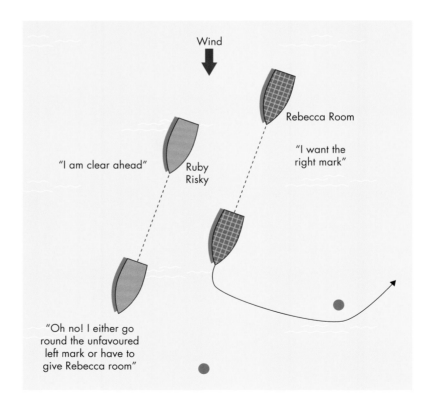

14.2a Rebecca Room and Ruby Risky

If you are not going to be the inside boat round the favoured mark consider your options.

(i) Slow down to get inside at the mark but behind with May Mark Rounding. This may mean an early spinnaker drop as soon as you are inside three boat lengths.

(ii) Sail fast and go around the outside if you want to foot left with Finlay Footing. This is more likely to be a viable option in strong winds if you can plane off underneath slower moving boats.

(iii) Go for the other mark if you want to avoid the other boats with Tilley Traffic. You will need to make your decision early as if you are nearly at the busy mark it might be a long sail to the other mark.

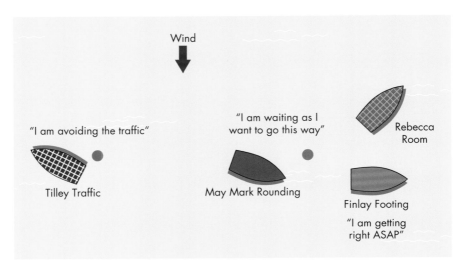

14.2b Tilley Traffic, May Mark Rounding, Finlay Footing and Rebecca Room take a different approach to the leeward gates.

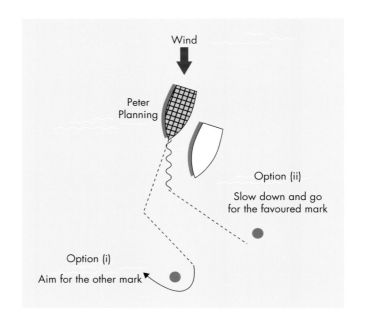

Wind

Peter
Planning

Option (ii)
Slow down and go
for the favoured mark

Option (i)
Aim for the other mark

14.2c Peter Planning looks at options when you are not inside boat

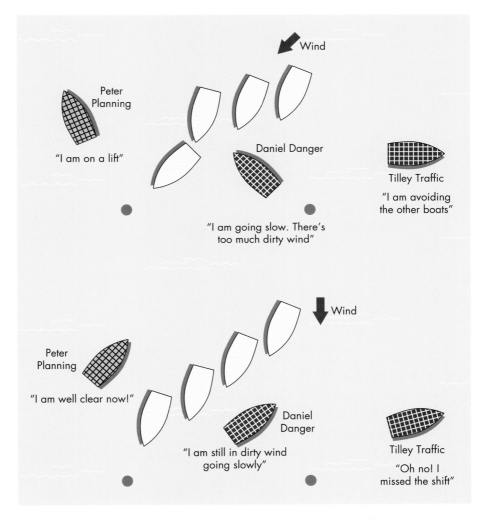

14.2d Sailing the shift with Daniel Danger, Peter Planning and Tilley Traffic

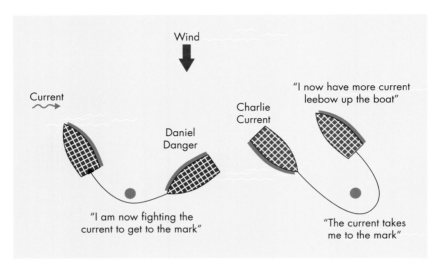

14.2e Charlie Current goes for the easiest downwind mark to get to, and has more of a leebow on the beat

In order to make the most of the shifts you must also consider the traffic, as sailing through the fleet in confused wind and water (and the possibility of collision) can be dangerous and may be worse than sailing on the wrong tack.

You also need to consider the tide, not only going into the most favourable/ avoiding the most adverse current, but if the current is across the course then this too will influence your choice of gates.

Remember you can break the overlap at the last moment if things are tight, like Oliver Overlap.

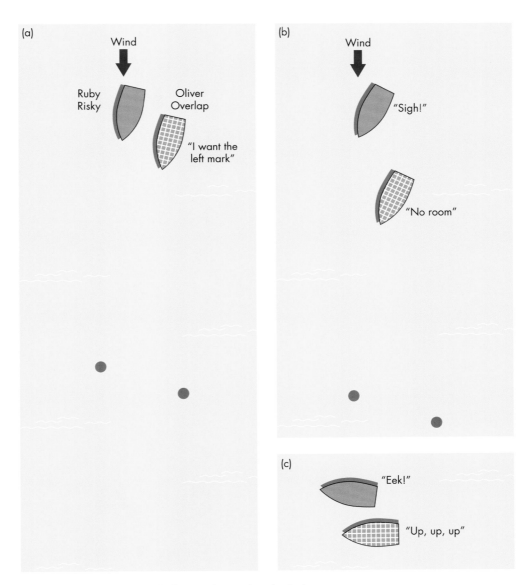

14.2f Oliver Overlap breaks his overlap with Ruby Risky

14.3   Sailing Aggressively

Remember the rules for rounding a mark apply at three boat lengths.

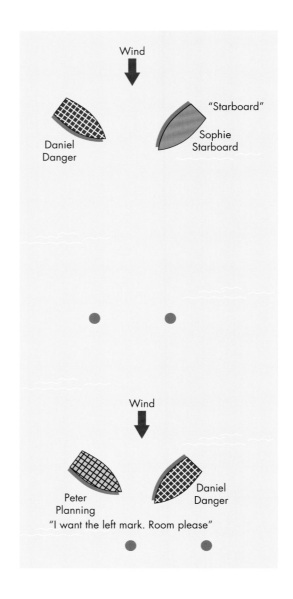

14.3a Daniel Danger gets caught out

Chapter 15
The Second Beat

The Difference between the First and Second Beat

Leverage

Controlling the Race

15.1   The Difference between the First and Second Beat

The main difference between the second beat and the first is that the fleet is more spread out, giving most boats more clean wind. Although this may still be an opportunity to take places, often it is a time to consolidate a good position. With the fleet more spread out you can concentrate more on speed and less on other boats. In other words set the boat up to go fast rather than be easy to race. See chapter 11 in *Be Your Own Sailing Coach.*

A good example of this was when I was doing some boat tuning work, long straight up rabbit runs, and boat A popped out in front every time. However we then did some short course windward leeward racing and boat B won every time. Both crews were of similar ability but one boat was set up for speed whereas the other had an easier set up which made it easier to tack and gybe and accelerate quickly but it had a slower top speed . . . a classic example of the difference between the first and the second beat. This is an example of changing gear. Boat A was in top gear whereas boat B was in fourth.

It is therefore not surprising that as soon as the lead boats get a little way ahead and stop "fighting" with each other they soon pull clear of the chasing pack. You can still loose cover the chasing pack but the important thing is to consider the fleet as a whole as a consistent series wins regattas.

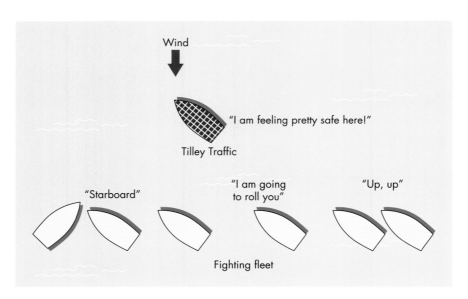

15.1a Tilley Traffic is launched!

15.2 Leverage

Generally the greater the potential gain the greater the risk. So like a game of poker you need to think carefully about how much you are willing to bet on your hand.

To make a gain on the fleet you need to do something different from the pack. Of course if you are happy with your current position (maybe you are first!) then you may simply want to defend your position (see Chapter 19 Attacking and Defending).

For example if you close cover someone by tacking on them every time (see Chapter 5 Tacking) you are zero potential gain and maybe a potential loss if the boat you are covering is unwilling to accept close cover and keeps tacking, slowing you both down. You should not simply fall into the habit of close covering the boat behind just because you don't think you can make any gains.

15.2a Lola Leverage (i) small leverage but gets it wrong (ii) large leverage and gets it right!

Remember you actually only convert your gain to windward when you tack and cross, so you can "bank" your winnings!

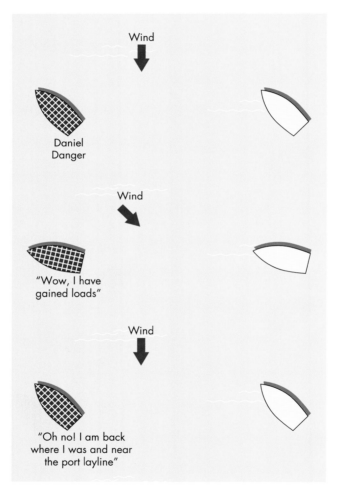

15.2b Daniel Danger makes a big gain but fails to bank it

15.3   Controlling the Race

Once you are in a good position you want to stay there! You need to consider what you would like the boats behind to do. If you are leading the race and the boats near you in the series are further back in the fleet, then you want the places to remain as they are and the race to finish as soon as possible, so you keep some boats between you and them. To extend your lead in the series, you would want to shepherd the fleet to the favoured side of the course.

If however you simply want to extend your lead in the race or make it difficult for those boats around you (perhaps they are close to you in the series), allowing other boats to come through, then you make it difficult for the boats close to you to go the favoured side of the course, which will make the race longer and allow more chances for place changes. Remember that if a boat is forced to defend its position from boats close to it, then it is unlikely it will be able to sail fast and present a threat to you.

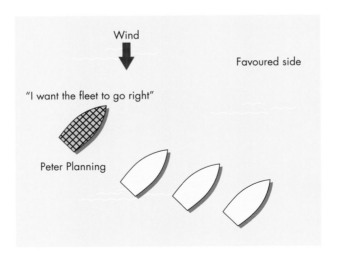

15.3a Peter Planning makes it easy for the boats behind to reach the favoured side

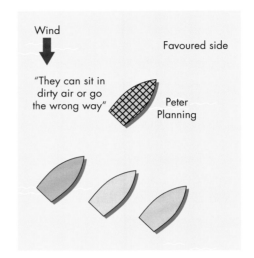

15.3b Peter Planning makes it hard for the boats behind to reach the favoured side

Chapter 16
The Final Beat

Long Final Beat
Short Final Beat
Dealing with Other Boats

16.1 Long Final Beat

A long final beat (upwind finish) is rare nowadays although some classes still do this, or perhaps a race officer will choose to shorten the course at the windward mark on the final race of the day in fading light or wind (or indeed if the wind is becoming unmanageably too strong) with an offshore wind (as this gives the shortest sail home).

By the final beat the fleet tends to be even more spread out but this is no time to relax. Place changes can and do happen, and don't underestimate the psychological advantage of finishing a race with a massive lead!

The tactics involved in a long final beat are much the same as the second beat. Loose cover any boats you need to (unless you are consciously trying to sail another boat down the fleet). You should be concentrating on speed and getting across the finish line. Remember your "position" is not safe until you cross that line and there are no guarantees in sailboat racing. Those boats miles in front of you could break something and you might still be able to overtake them before the finish.

If you are well clear of the boats behind and just want to defend your position with no particular bias to the beat then sail for approximately half the distance you are ahead, tack and sail for the other half. Then watch the boats behind: if they tack go with them. If they don't tack, tack back to loose cover. This means you are not vulnerable to windshifts.

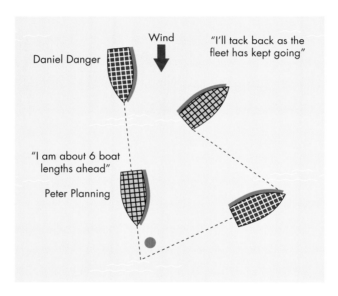

16.1a Peter Planning protects his position

16.2   Short Final Beat

The short final beat usually becomes very much about the finish. You need to consider which end of the finish line and indeed which tack you are going to finish on before you round the leeward mark (see Chapter 17 The Finish).

It is often very hard to gain places as due to the length of the leg it is difficult to get enough leverage. Instead you need to concentrate on not making unnecessary losses through doing lots of extra tacks or sitting in too much dirty wind.

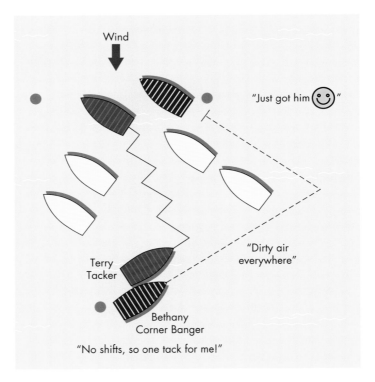

16.2a Terry Tacker does too many tacks

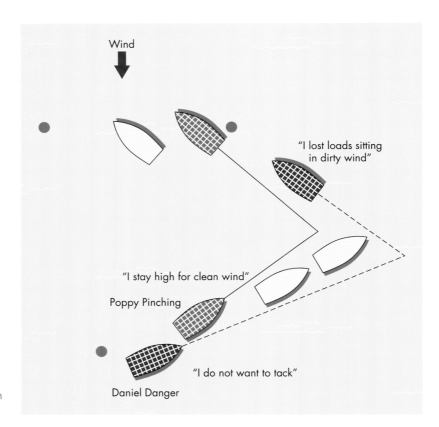

16.2b Daniel Danger sitting in dirty wind

In addition you must consider that you are trying to get through an upwind gate. Here the current has a huge effect.

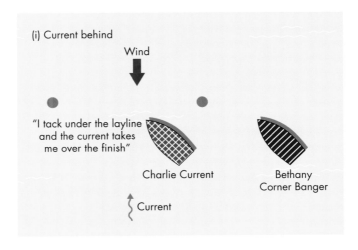

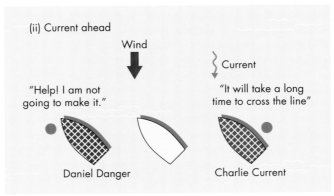

16.2c Charlie Current allows for the current perfectly: (i) current behind (ii) current ahead

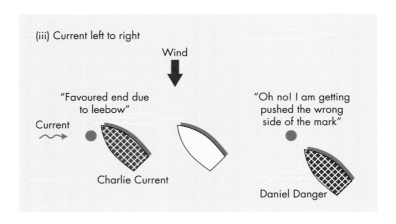

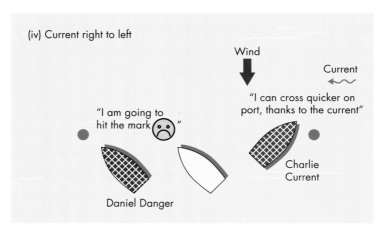

16.2c (Continued) (iii) current left to right (iv) current right to left

16.3   Dealing with Other Boats

Keep going! Other sailors may well be tired and mistakes do happen. You want to be in a position to take advantage of these. Don't simply split tack unless you have nothing to lose.

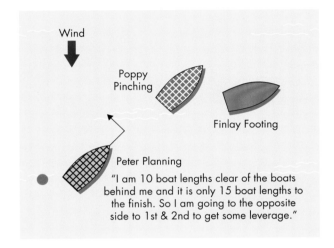

Wind

Poppy
Pinching

Finlay Footing

Peter Planning

"I am 10 boat lengths clear of the boats behind me and it is only 15 boat lengths to the finish. So I am going to the opposite side to 1st & 2nd to get some leverage."

16.3a Peter Planning splits from the boats ahead as he is well clear

It is important that you do not allow boats to control you. So as someone tacks to cover you want to time your tack so you can break away. Make sure they are really tacking (not doing a dummy tack) then aim to complete your tack at the same time. You can then foot to get away from them as quickly as possible.

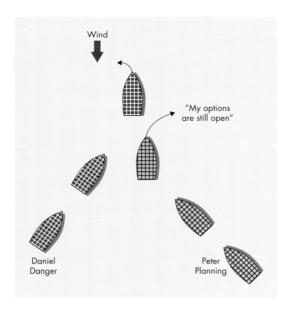

16.3b Peter Planning avoids the covering tack

The easiest way to control someone is to sail them to the layline.

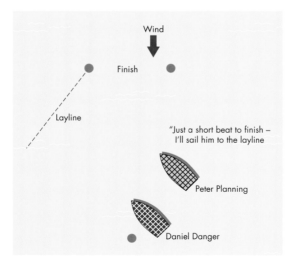

16.3c Peter Planning takes control

Chapter 17
The Finish

The Basics
After the Finish
Dealing with Other Boats

17.1 The Basics

Always watch out for the shortened course flag!

Don't relax until you have finished. In fact on a windy day don't relax until the boat is tied on its trolley, ashore and with the sails down and rolled. It can be very disappointing to have a breakage as a result of a capsize after the racing for the day is finished.

Top tips for finishing (where possible):

- Finish at the favoured end of the line (that which is most downwind for an upwind finish and the most upwind for a downwind finish).

- Finish on the tack which goes most directly across the line. The favoured tack to cross the line may well mean you need to tack at the favoured end of the line if the line is not square. For example you may finish at the port end on port.

- In some conditions it may pay to dip (where you go head to wind for an upwind finish or dead downwind for a downwind finish).

You have finished when any part of the boat in its normal sailing position crosses the line. If dipping you need to time it perfectly, usually changing your angle at the last moment so as to directly cross the line. You do not have to completely cross the finish.

See examples of Frederick Finish finishing:

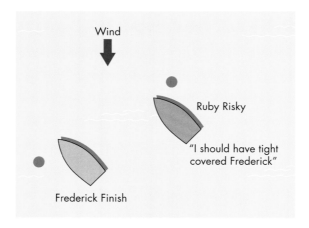

17.1a Frederick finishes at the favoured end

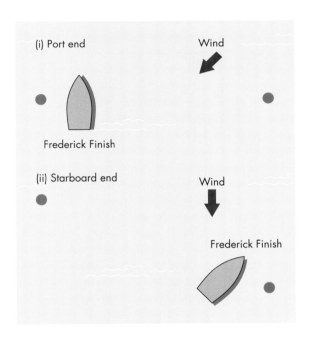

17.1b Frederick finishes on the favoured tack (i) port end (ii) starboard end

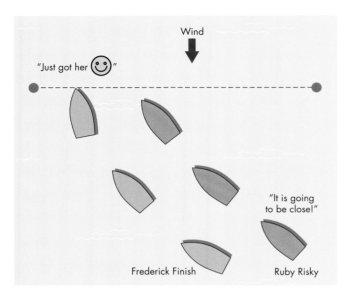

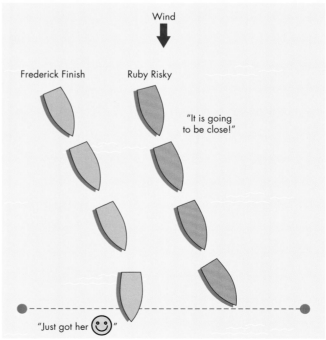

17.1c Frederick dips to finish

17.2 After the Finish

When you have finished there are no longer penalties for infringing unless you infringe a boat that is still racing (has yet to finish). Normally you would continue sailing in the way that helps you clear the line as soon as possible. Now is a good time to refuel and rehydrate and have a nice positive debrief. Remember if you have not sailed the correct course you can still go back (even after the finish) and sail the correct course.

17.3 Dealing with Other Boats

When dealing with other boats you need to keep your options open. As a windward boat with room at a mark it is usually a good idea to hail to make sure the other boat gives you room. However in an ideal world you would be approaching on a layline to the finish (not over the layline).

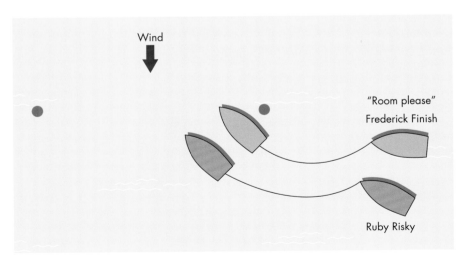

17.3a Frederick gets room to finish

A windward boat must keep clear of a leeward boat unless taking room to finish. This means the leeward boat can go up to head to wind to cross the line.

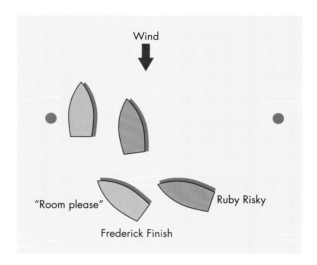

However a leeward boat can not force a windward boat to tack unless the windward boat has to tack to finish. This means if the windward boat dips the line you

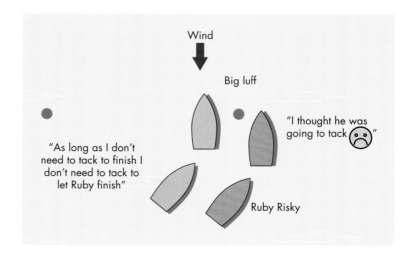

could end up the wrong side of it yourself. However if he needs to tack you can ask for room to tack. If he does not give it to you and you have to tack to finish then you can protest.

Remember if you do infringe you need to take your penalty as soon as possible and refinish. If you hit a mark you need to do one gybe and one tack and if you infringe a boat you need to do two gybes and two tacks. You also need to sail completely to the course side before finishing.

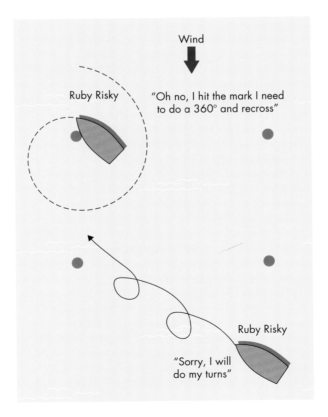

17.3d Ruby Risky takes her penalty

Chapter 18
Being Consistent

The Basics

Have a Plan

Avoiding High Risks

18.1 The Basics

Being consistent is especially important in big fleets as a small error can result in the loss of many places. You need good decision making, rather than simply seeing what happens, which may work in a smaller fleet if your speed is good but when you get to an international regatta you will find the majority of the fleet are fast!

Never get let down by your boatwork. There are usually many signs of wear and tear before items actually fail. When you wash your boat down, check it over thoroughly to see if anything needs to be repaired or replaced.

Plan well ahead so you have done lots of training before your key regattas and have good boatspeed (a fast boat turns you into a tactical genius!) and can rely on your boat handling skills in pressure situations. You should have already used *Be Your Own Sailing Coach* to establish any goals which need working on well before your key regatta.

You should be aware of the regatta venue and what the key factors are likely to be. Has the venue got strong tide? A good chance of sea breeze? A large area of very high ground which bends the wind or consistently flatter water in one area of the course (may be due to depth of water)? Being aware of these things will make it easier to take quick decisions in a race as you know what you can expect to happen.

Keep out of trouble. Races are won by sailing fast and pointing the boat in the right direction, not by "beating" every other boat in the fleet. Remember it really does not help you if you were the right of way boat and you end up being sunk! If trouble does find you never give up. One of the best things about sailboat racing is that however bad the situation seems things can always turn around!

Near the end of the regatta you can decide how much risk to take. For example if you have to win the last race to win the regatta and you are guaranteed second place, then you would have a less conservative strategy (perhaps going further into the favoured side of the course) than if there were lots of boats close on points with you and you had to count the last race (and couldn't afford a bad result).

Key ideas:

- You do not (and should not, due to rule 14) hit another boat to prove it broke a rule.

- It may not be necessary under the rules to hail but it can help avoid a possible collision.

- Whatever happens, get on with the race (do your turns, protest or do turns and protest). Don't waste concentration that could be making you go faster, in having a shouting match.

However if there is an incident here are the key ideas for the protest room:

- You can protest an incident that affected you (you can protest and take a penalty) or one that you witnessed.

- Do not get into a detailed discussion with the boats ashore. Just ask any witness what they saw (so you can judge whether it will help your case and get the protest form completed using as few words as possible (to make it clear).

- In the hearing be precise and polite. State what happened and when. Keep the words simple and consistent (I asked for room at three boat lengths) and listen to the other party's case so you can ask questions. At the end come up with a clear and concise summary (don't just repeat everything you have just said).

18.2 Have a Plan

Have a plan, have a back up plan – in fact have two or more!

The key is to stay calm and think rationally. You may have to bite the bullet and change what you want to do but you can never affect what has happened, you can only influence the future. Work out what is the most significant factor (clean air for example) and work on it. If you are having problems concentrating (maybe due to stress) focus on one thing (the most important – perhaps keeping the boat flat) and then it will be easier to concentrate on others (perhaps steering better).

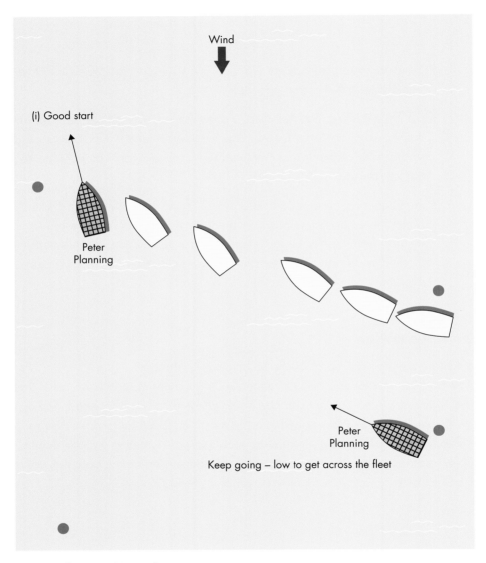

Wind

(i) Good start

Peter
Planning

Peter
Planning

Keep going – low to get across the fleet

18.2a Peter Planning: (i) Good start

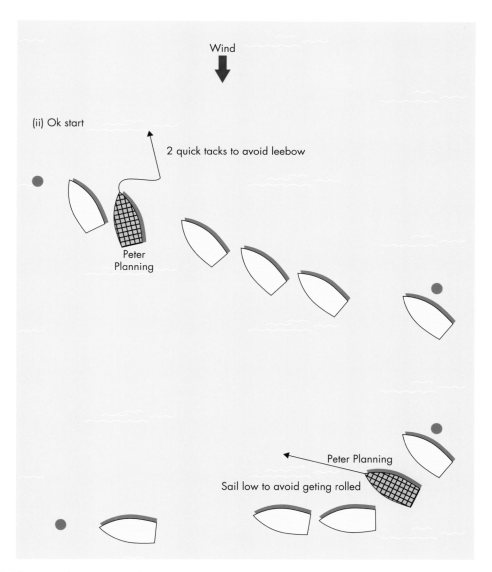

Wind

(ii) Ok start

2 quick tacks to avoid leebow

Peter
Planning

Peter Planning

Sail low to avoid geting rolled

18.2b Peter Planning: (ii) Ok start

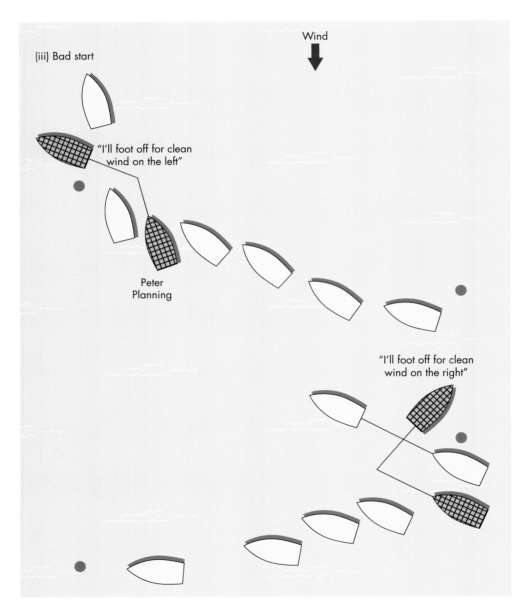

18.2c Peter Planning: (iii) Bad start

Know your priorities: is going the right way more important? Or is clean air? Could this change? For example if the wind is light, clean air may be most important but in 25 knots going the correct way may be crucial. Bear this in mind if the conditions change (for example a front comes through or a thermal breeze kicks in).

Damage limitation: if you are unable to avoid sailing in dirty air then try and limit the damage. If the boat in front is well forward and you are unlikely to be able to sail through the dirty air consider pinching up to clean your wind.

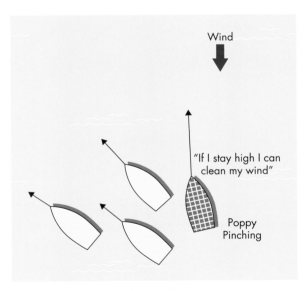

18.2b Poppy Pinching avoids slipping into further dirty air

However if the boat is more to windward then you need to foot like Finlay to clean your wind as soon as possible.

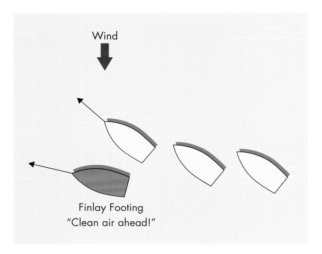

Wind

Finlay Footing
"Clean air ahead!"

18.2c Finlay Footing gets clean air as soon as possible

If it all goes wrong don't be tempted to just bang a corner as you can make the situation worse – keep a clear head and keep making the small gains. You would only want to do this if you really were last and there was nothing to lose! What ever happens you NEVER retire (unless of course your boat is so broken you can not get it over the finish line) as you have no idea what is going to happen later on in the regatta and you don't want to have to count any letters (OCS, DSQ, DNF, RTD etc.) in your final points!

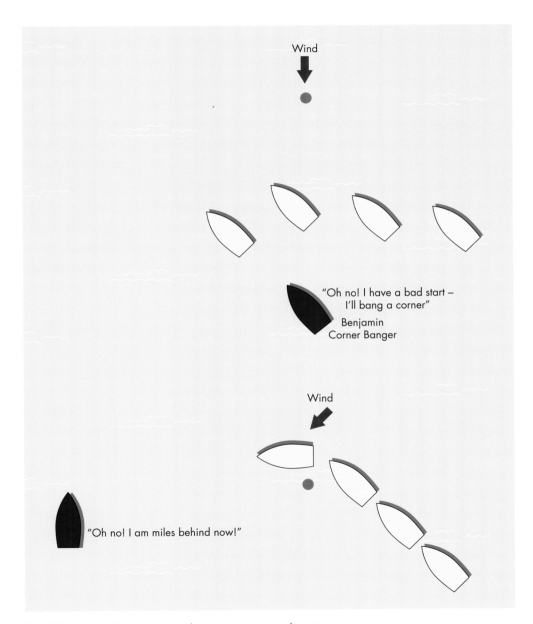

18.2d Benjamin Corner Banger bangs a corner making it worse

18.3 Avoiding High Risks

Avoid danger areas! Unless you are well clear of all the other boats there are certain "kill zones" on the race course such as:

- Centre of the start line in light winds as if you had a bad start it is hard to get out and get clean wind. Avoid this unless you are confident of a good start and you trust your transits!

- Hitting the laylines too early. There is usually a slow procession of boats all stuffing each other up and slowing each other down, especially in light winds. The further away you get from the mark the more likely boats are to have overstood the mark as they all tack very slightly to windward and give you dirty wind which you can not avoid since you are on the layline or you have to massively overstand yourself.

- However you can not arrive too late or there may not be a gap for you to tack into. Watch the fleet carefully. If you are just below the layline duck out early, sail through a gap (there is usually room as long as you are three or more boat lengths from the mark). Just tack as soon as possible to minimise overstand.

- Tacking inside the three boat length circle is a definite no-no as the chance of infringing another boat is high, or if you duck you could end up having to duck many, many boats before you find a gap.

- Where you can, make the boat handling as easy as possible to prevent errors unless there is a large gain to be had. For example it is much easier (and likely quicker) to round the left hand leeward gate on starboard and carry on than to come into the right hand gate on starboard, gybe and drop the kite at the mark, then tack straight after it.

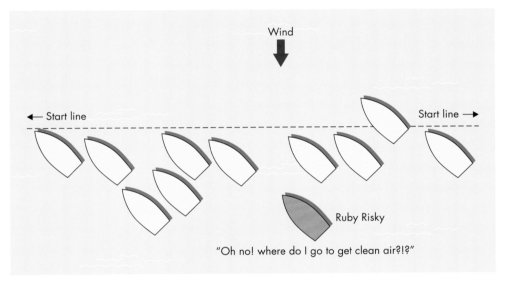

18.3a Ruby Risky starting in the centre of a long start line

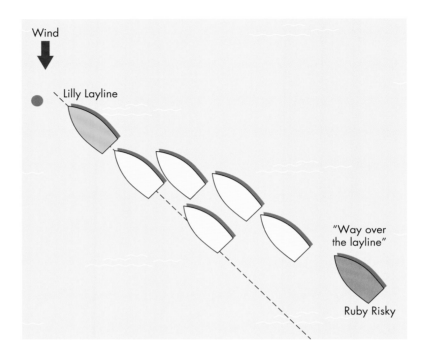

18.3b Ruby Risky hits the layline too early and overstands

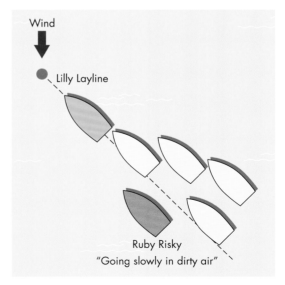

18.3c Ruby Risky misses the layline and sits in dirty air

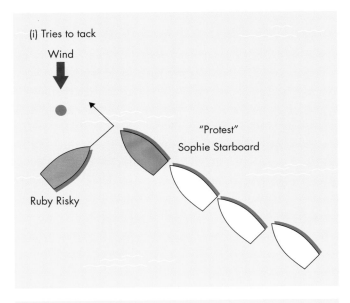

(i) Tries to tack

Wind

"Protest"
Sophie Starboard

Ruby Risky

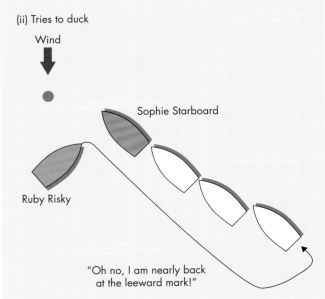

(ii) Tries to duck

Wind

Sophie Starboard

Ruby Risky

"Oh no, I am nearly back
at the leeward mark!"

18.3d Ruby Risky hits the layline too late and (i) Tries to tack, (ii) Tries to duck

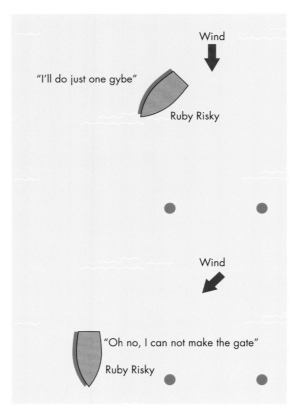

18.3e Ruby Risky misses the gate downwind

Chapter 19
Attacking and Defending

When Should I Attack and Defend?
Specific Manoeuvres Upwind
Specific Manoeuvres Downwind

19.1   When Should I Attack and Defend?

It rarely pays to concentrate on beating one boat as the 98 or so are getting away sailing their own race. However there are key areas of the race course or regatta when this is necessary so the ability to attack and defend is a vital tool to have in the tool box and one which can be worked on by practising match and team racing skills. Here are some of the key areas:

- At the start – you have no options until you pop out the front (or fall behind). So you need to concentrate on beating the boats around you.

- When boats meet you will have no choice but to react to them and whether you cross, tack or duck can have long-term implications for the race.

- When there is a specific boat you have to beat in a race or series. Here you defend the boat to windward by sailing high. This way they do not have the room to roll you and if they are forced to tack off you have a clear lane to tack into when you want.

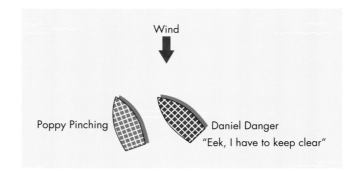

19.1a Poppy Pinching

You could also attack boats to leeward by driving over the top of them if you have enough bow forward and space to leeward.

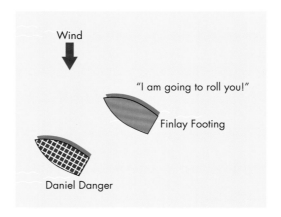

19.1b Finlay Footing

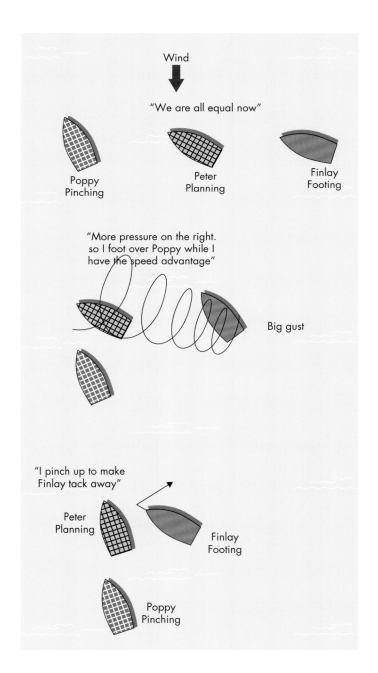

19.1c Peter Planning uses both footing and pinching to beat the boats around him

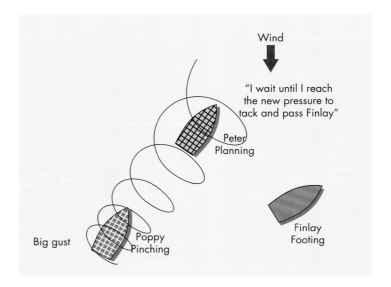

Wind

"I wait until I reach
the new pressure to
tack and pass Finlay"

Peter
Planning

Big gust

Poppy
Pinching

Finlay
Footing

19.1c (Continued)

19.2   Specific Manoeuvres Upwind

Leo Leebow is the expert at leebowing. This is an important manoeuvre to get
right – get it wrong and you get rolled (like Daniel) which means you not only have to
tack back to your original tack (costing you the distance you lose doing two tacks) but
you will also be going slower than you were before you did two tacks.

Use the leebow when you want to protect the side of the course. You should not
always leebow. There may be times when it is better simply to allow the other boat to
cross if you believe they are going the wrong way!

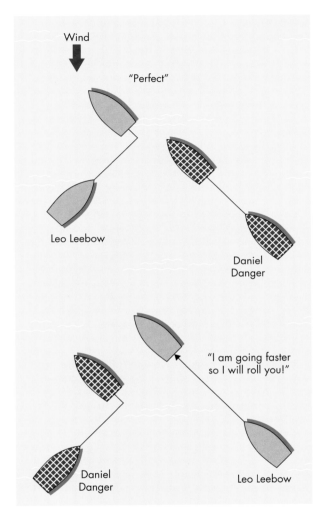

19.2a Leo Leebow and Daniel Danger

In order to stop boats tacking in at the layline bear away to close the gap (three boat lengths). They will either duck you or tack early. Either way you head up like Leo Leebow and are safe.

If however you are not on the layline, you need to tack as the boat ducks you to stay in control.

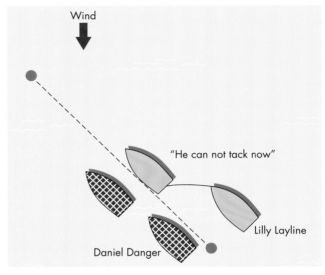

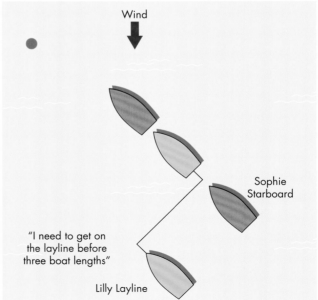

Of course one of the simplest ways to attack, especially if you are a few boat lengths ahead, is simply to cover (the further you are in front the less the effect of your wind shadow). You can either slow them down slightly with dirty wind or force them to sail away from the favoured side of the course to maintain clear wind.

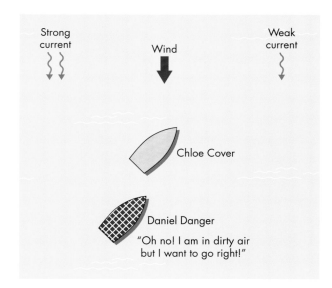

19.2c Loose covering with Chloe Cover

19.3   Specific Manoeuvres Downwind

For many classes of boat pressure downwind is usually the key factor (for a start, shifts happen less frequently downwind as you are sailing away from them – you are sailing towards them when going upwind!)

On a run it rarely pays to gybe set if there is a spacer mark, as the dirty wind caused by the boats reaching can be serious bad news unless you are well clear of the pack. So you would not worry if an attacking boat took this route and you would think twice about defending it unless you were only worried about this one boat or confident this was the way you wanted to go. It would be better to wait until later in the leg to make your move.

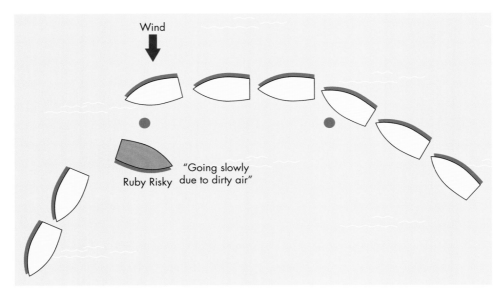

19.3a Ruby Risky risks sailing in bad wind

The easiest way to pass a boat is often to work high in a lull then drive down hard in the gust. By the time the defender realises it should be too late and you are through. Don't go high unless you expect a large change in wind speed otherwise you may simply end up taking you both high (unless this is what you want).

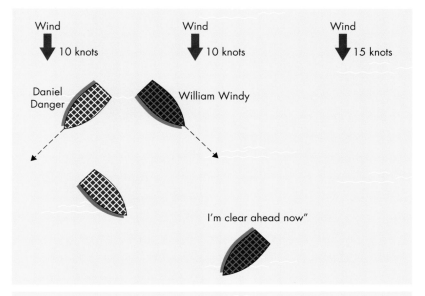

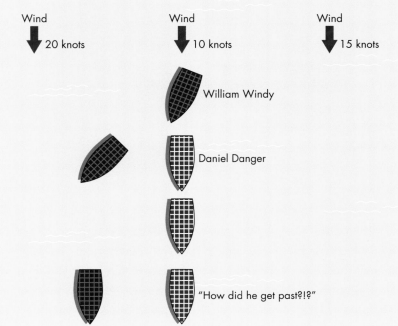

19.3b William Windy gets the jump on Daniel Danger

Of course you can get underneath but this is usually more a case of working the other boat up and then gaining an overlap, as it can be very hard to break through underneath a boat of the same class which is going a similar speed.

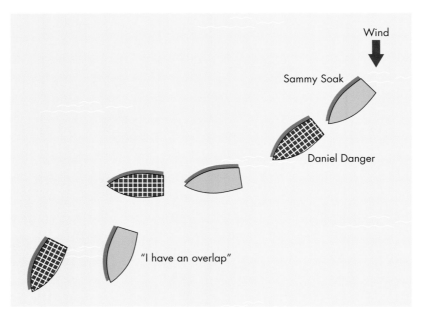

19.3c Sammy Soak breaks through downwind

The easiest way to get clear of another boat is to gybe off and sail your own race like Tilley Traffic but if you want to attack a specific boat you would want to gybe right on their face. Here you take control of the situation and gybe right when they do . . . this is why good boat handling skills are a must. You may need to soak into position like Sammy Soak or you may have just gybed off like Tilley and made a small gain and gybed back. This works well with asymmetric kites.

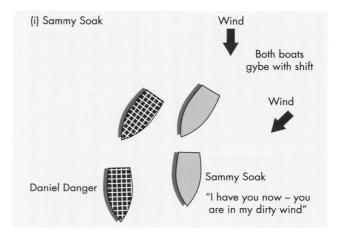

19.3d
Overtaking by gybing with (i) Sammy Soak and (ii) Tilley Traffic

Of course if someone is trying to gybe on you, you need to make your gybe slick (top crews do not give any signals they are going to gybe). They get the boat going high and up to full speed (breaking any cover asap).

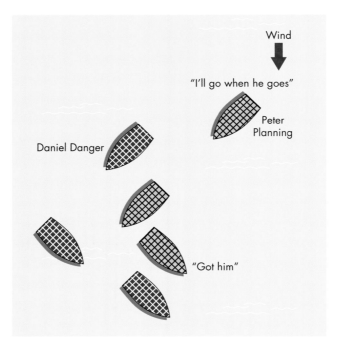

19.3e Peter Planning waits for the best opportunity to gybe

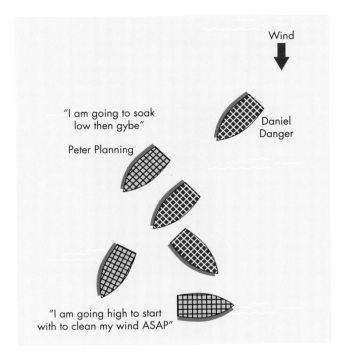

19.3e (Continued)

Just like sailing upwind you can use covering to great effect downwind, especially in symmetrical spinnaker boats, forcing them to either sail high, sit in dirty wind or gybe to the unfavoured side of the course.

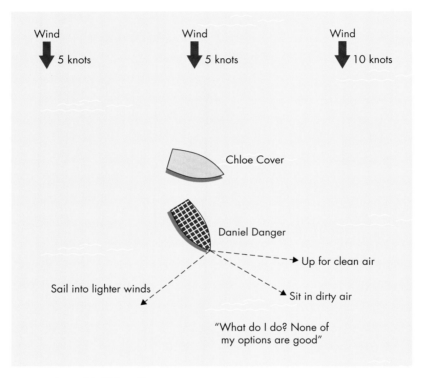

19.3f Loose covering with Chloe Cover

Chapter 20
Weather

Forecasts
Using the Weather
Thermal and Sea Breezes

20.1 Forecasts

Florence Forecast always has a plan and this is based on having the appropriate information available. Sailing is a dynamic sport: there are loads of variables, most of them completely beyond your control (which is part of what makes the sport so exciting but also what can make it rather frustrating at times). One of these key variables is the weather.

Having a good source of weather information is very important. If you always use the same sources then you will learn if they tend to over- or underestimate for various venues or perhaps systems tend to come in sooner or later than expected. The more recent a forecast the more accurate it is likely to be.

Here are some good sites:

www.windguru.cz
www.metoffice.gov.uk

Many places will also have live weather information so you can check how closely conditions are reflecting the forecast, for example:

www.weather-file.com/portland/

Lastly, don't forget you can get up-to-date tidal information. A good site is:

www.easytide.co.uk

To learn more about Meteorology see chapter 10 in *Be Your Own Sailing Coach*.

20.2   Using the Weather

Depressions (a small low pressure feature) crossing can have a profound effect on the race. You will often hear the term "cyclonic" referred to in shipping forecasts. Here the wind direction is anticlockwise and slightly towards the centre of the low in the northern hemisphere.

Obviously the position relative to the path of the depression in the northern hemisphere will affect what happens to you and can be seen by Florence Forecast:

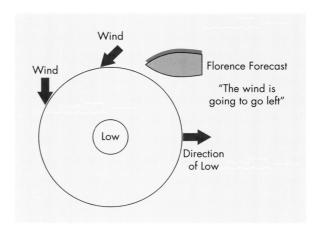

20.2a Florence Forecast north of a depression

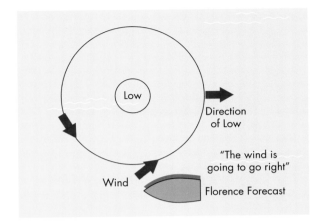

20.2b Florence Forecast south of a depression

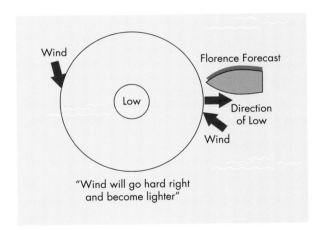

20.2c Florence Forecast in direct path of a depression

In the southern hemisphere things are reversed (the wind is going clockwise in a low pressure).

Low pressures tend to move more quickly than high pressures which can be very static especially in the summer time. The flow of wind in a northern hemisphere high pressure is (clockwise) opposite to that of a low pressure, but since they tend to move slowly they are much less likely to influence you during the course of a race.

20.3   Thermal and Sea Breezes

A thermal breeze is where the land heats up in relation to the water, when the wind is onshore. This may be because during the course of the day the sun has warmed the land or it may be a change in water temperature as the tide turns.

Here (in the northern hemisphere) unless the breeze was quite strong to begin with you would expect the wind to decrease within around four miles of the coast line with the wind slowly veering. If the wind is already to the right, looking offshore, then there may be a slight bend. However as the wind decreases, pressure across the course will be very different, so staying in pressure is the key to winning races.

A sea breeze starts when the land heats up in relation to the water, when the wind is offshore. There is usually an area of very light or no wind before the sea breeze fully fills in. The right side of the course will nearly always pay when this happens (the sea breeze extends all the way to the shoreline and has burnt off any low mist). The breeze will go right, throughout the afternoon (it would go left in the southern hemisphere).

The diagrams below show a south facing coast in the northern hemisphere but they could easily represent a west facing coast for example by rotating them 90 degrees clockwise. Likewise for the southern hemisphere the effects are the opposite.

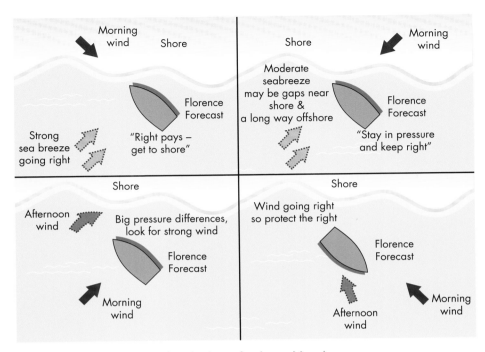

20.3a Florence Forecast makes the best of a thermal/sea breeze

Glossary

Abandon.   A race which the race committee declares to be void, not counted in the series, but may be resailed.

Apparent wind.   The actual flow of air acting upon the sail, or the wind as it appears to the sailor. If the boat were stationary, the true and apparent wind would be the same. However as a boat increases in speed, the apparent wind becomes progressively faster and further forward than the true wind.

Back.   The wind turning in an anti-clockwise direction.

Banging the corner.   To sail right to the edge of one side of the race course.

Bear away.   To change course away from the wind.

Bias.   The end of the line which is the closest to the next mark, or in the case of the finish, the end of the line which is closest to the last mark you passed.

Black Flag.   If a black flag has been displayed, no part of a boat's hull, crew or equipment shall be in the triangle formed by the ends of the starting line and the first mark during the minute before her starting signal. If a boat breaks this rule and is identified, she shall be disqualified without a hearing, even if the race is restarted, resailed or rescheduled, but not if it is postponed or abandoned before the starting signal.

Breeze.   Wind.

Chop.   The short steep waves which can have a dramatic effect on reducing boat speed. In these conditions it may pay to foot.

Converging   Describes the wind off the land and the wind off the sea coming nearer together.

Cover loose.   To position yourself so you are going the same way as another boat to protect your lead should there be a wind shift etc.

Cover tight.   To position yourself between another boat and the wind, to give maximum dirty air.

Cross.   To pass in front of another boat.

Current.   The flow of water in a particular direction.

Death roll.   A movement of the boat where the flow of wind continually switches direction across the sail, causing the boat to roll to windward, then to leeward and back again, often resulting in a capsize.

Diverging.   The action of the wind off the land and the wind off the sea moving further apart.

Duck.   To pass behind another boat.

Exonerate.   To take a penalty for breaking a racing rule. A boat may for example complete penalty turn(s) or retire from the race.

Favoured side.   The side which enables you to get to the next mark in the shortest possible time.

Finish.   The imaginary line which you cross (with any part of your boat in a normal sailing position) to end the race.

Footing.   When a boat sailing upwind points as low (as far away from upwind) as possible while still maximising ground made to windward.

Get water.   One boat is given room by another boat to allow her to pass a mark or obstruction.

Going high.   Sailing upwind of the straight line to the next mark.

Going low.   Sailing downwind of the straight line to the next mark.

Gust.   An area of stronger wind which is travelling downwind and often fanning out (as opposed to pressure which stays in one place). To take advantage of gusts you want to maximise the amount of time spent in them.

Gybe.   To change the side of the sail which fills with wind to the other side when you are sailing downwind.

Gybe set.   To gybe and set the spinnaker on a new tack.

Headed tack.   The tack where a boat has to bear away (to keep the same sail settings) as a result of a change in wind direction.

Header.   A header is where the wind direction changes (heads), forcing the boat to bear away to keep the sail settings the same.

Keeping clear.   To allow another boat to sail her course with no need to take avoiding action. When boats are overlapped on the same tack this means the leeward boat can change course in both directions without immediately making contact with the windward boat.

Kite.   Another name for spinnaker.

Lane.   The line you sail to keep your wind free from turbulence from other boats.

Lay line.   The lay line is the straight line which will allow a boat to round the windward mark in the shortest possible time without tacking. This is affected by wind speed, direction and current flows.

Lee bowed.   You are lee bowed by a boat close to leeward giving you dirty wind.

Leeward   (pronounced "loo-erd"). A boat's leeward side is the side that is (or when she is head to wind, was) away from the wind. However, when sailing by the lee or directly downwind, her leeward side is the side on which her mainsail lies. The other side is her windward side. When two boats on the same tack overlap, the one on the leeward side of the other is the leeward boat. The other is the windward boat.

Leverage.   How far you position yourself away from other boats to make a gain. The further away you are the bigger the lever (the greater the potential gain/loss).

Lifted tack.   The lifted tack is the tack where a boat has to head up (to keep the same sail settings) as a result of a change in wind direction.

Lifting.   Where the wind direction changes (lifts), forcing the boat to head up to keep the same sail settings.

Luffing.   To go towards where the wind is coming from.

Mean wind.   The average wind in terms of speed and direction.

OCS.   On Course Side. For any part of a boat being on the race course side (OCS) prior to the start. You will have to restart the race, may incur a penalty or possibly be disqualified.

Offshore breeze.   A breeze which is coming off the shore (from the land).

Onshore breeze.   A breeze which is coming off the land (from the water).

Oscillating breeze.   A breeze which is regularly swinging to the left and right (perhaps going to the left for 5 minutes, mean wind direction for 5 minutes, right for 5 minutes, back to mean wind direction for 5 minutes and so forth).

Overlap.   An overlap is established when one boat on the same tack as another has a part of her, in normal sailing position, over the line abeam from the back of the other. (So for example overlap can exist between a spinnaker pole and a rudder, but boat lengths refer only to the length of the hulls – not including spinnaker poles etc).

Overstanding.   When a boat is to windward of the layline. This results in her taking a greater time than necessary to reach the windward mark.

Pin end.   The port end of the start or finish line, often a buoy.

Pinching (pointing).   A boat sailing upwind pointing as high (as close to upwind as possible) whilst still maximising ground made to windward.

Postpone.   To delay before the scheduled start. Such a race could subsequently be started or abandoned.

Pressure.   The amount of wind constantly over a piece of water. For example there may be constantly more wind on the left hand side of the course than the right. This is different from gusts (which move).

Racing.   The time you are sailing, from the preparatory signal until the finish when you clear the finishing line or retire (or until the race committee signal a general recall, postponement or abandonment).

Recall. When one or more identified boats are recalled to the starting area (individual recall) or when a race is restarted (general recall).

Rolling. When a boat heels to windward then to leeward and back again (or vice versa).

Room. The space (water) which must be allowed for a boat to sail to the mark, and then room to sail her proper course while at the mark. However room at the mark does not include room to tack unless the boat is overlapped to windward and is on the inside of the boat required to give room.

Round Robin. A race series where everyone is divided into groups of approximately equal numbers and abilities. Each group then races the other groups (ideally once and then the group members are changed on the basis of that day's results ready for the next day's racing).

Sailing by the lee. To sail downwind when the flow of wind across the sail is from the leech to the luff of the sail (so the telltales fly towards the mast).

Sailing over. To pass someone to windward. You are rolled when a boat to windward gives you dirty wind.

Sailing under. To pass someone to leeward.

Sausage course. A windward/leeward course. If you draw a line around the course you would sail (ignoring tacks and gybes), it looks like a sausage! (See course diagrams at the back of the book.)

Sea breeze. An onshore breeze generated by the difference in the temperature between the land and the sea.

Shift. A change in wind direction.

Shifty breeze. A breeze constantly changing direction with no pattern, perhaps caused by the wind coming over some high land or going round tall trees or buildings.

SI. Sailing Instructions. The rules of a specific championship, series or race.

Slam dunk. To tack right on top of someone, giving them the maximum amount of dirty air in a position where they can not immediately tack off.

Soak.   The boat is sailed downwind pointing low (pointing as close to dead downwind as possible) whilst still maximising ground made to leeward.

Start.   The imaginary line which you cross (with any part of your boat in a normal sailing position) after the starting signal to start the race.

Strategy.   The way you would sail around a course as quickly as possible in the absence of other boats.

Swell.   Long rolling waves which do not break. These can often be surfed downwind.

Tack.   To change from port to starboard or vice versa with the front of the boat passing through the wind. A boat's tack is defined by her windward side.

Tactics.   The way you react to the boats around you.

Telltales.   Pieces of wool or ribbon attached to the sail or stay to indicate the wind direction.

Tides.   The rising (flooding) and falling (ebbing) of Earth's ocean surface twice each day caused by the tidal forces of the moon and the sun acting on the oceans.

Topography.   The shape and surface of the surrounding area.

Transit.   A line going through two fixed points.

Veer.   The term used to describe the wind turning in a clockwise direction.

VMG.   Velocity Made Good. The total distance travelled in a certain direction in a certain time.

Wind bend.   A gradual change in the wind direction, often caused by topography.

Windward.   A boat's windward side is the side that is (or when she is head to wind, was) towards the wind. However, when sailing by the lee or directly downwind, her windward side is the opposite side to which her mainsail lies. The other side is her leeward side. When two boats on the same tack overlap, the one on the windward side of the other is the windward boat. The other is the leeward boat.

Index of Boat Names

Alfie Average Alfie sails an average angle downwind.

Archie Arc Archie sails far more distance than he needs to downwind, sailing a huge arc rather than going straight to the next mark.

Ava Accelerate Ava is very good at accelerating and she practises, so that she knows just how long it will take her to get up to full speed.

Ben Bias Ben always goes for the biased end (the one which is the most upwind when starting or finishing downwind, the one most downwind when finishing upwind or starting downwind).

Benjamin and Bethany Corner Bangers Benjamin and Bethany are brother and sister who sail right to the corners of the race course rather than tacking to take advantage of changing conditions. Benjamin Bethany

Brooke Big Fleet Brooke is an expert at sailing in big fleets and does as many national regattas (across several classes) as she can to gain experience.

Charlie Current Charlie Current is always keen to maximise his tidal advantage compared to other boats.

Charlotte Cross Charlotte is slightly ahead and so can cross the boats around her.

Chloe Cover Chloe uses her wind shadow to slow other boats down.

Daisy Duck Daisy will duck a starboard boat to carry on the way she wants to go.

Daniel Danger Daniel allows himself to get into a position where he could easily get rolled.

Finlay Footing Finlay likes to sail the boat fast and free upwind, bearing the boat away as much as possible without losing velocity made good (vmg) towards the windward mark.

Florence Forecast Florence always gets a very accurate forecast so that she knows what to expect and can use it to her best advantage on race day.

Frederick Finish The race is not over until it is over! Frederick is an expert finisher and can often grab those vital few places at the last possible moment.

Freya Favoured Side Freya always tries to get to the favoured side of the course, considering the big picture.

Gabriel Gybe Set Gabriel always immediately gybes and sets the spinnaker at the windward mark.

Garry Gyber Garry is an expert gyber whatever class of boat he is in.

George Greedy You are only allowed to take so much room to round the mark, George!

Georgia Gust Georgia takes maximum advantage of the gusts by sailing low in them, then coming back up in the lulls.

Harriet Header Unfortunately Harriet's wind awareness is not always spot on so she often sails upwind on a header.

Harry High Harry sails as high as he can downwind without losing velocity made good (vmg) to the leeward mark. This is good for rolling over boats.

Layla Lane Layla Lane holds her lane so she can sail in clean wind the way she wants to go.

Leo Leebow Leo likes to leebow other boats, forcing them to either tack off or fall behind.

Lewis Lee Lewis sails a single hander with an unstayed rig and likes to sail by the lee.

Lilly Layline Lilly is an expert at getting the laylines spot on, not arriving too late, too early or too far over or under.

Lola Leverage Lola uses leverage to pass the fleet but she is a good gambler, only getting lots of leverage when she knows she is going the right way.

Lucas Low Lucas sails as low as he can downwind without losing velocity made good (vmg) to the leeward mark. This is good for soaking under boats.

May Mark Rounding May always does a good mark rounding even if it means she has to slow down and follow round behind an ahead boat.

Oliver Overlap Oliver changes the angle of his boat wherever possible to make and break overlaps. Remember the overlap is on any part of the boat in its normal sailing position (for example spinnaker pole or rudder).

Peter Planning Peter always has a plan and a back up plan and another back up plan! Sailing is a very dynamic sport and it always pays to be prepared!

Poppy Pinching Poppy likes to sail the boat as high (close to the wind) as possible, always trying to head up as much as she can without losing velocity made good (vmg) towards the windward mark.

Rebecca Room Rebecca Room is an expert at getting room at the mark and when Rebecca has to give room she gives just seaman like rounding for the inside boat.

Riley Rounding A good rounding is nice and smooth so you exit the mark with your "racing line". This means you have a lane in front of you where you can sail without being in dirty wind.

Ruby Risky Ruby puts herself in areas of the race course which are best avoided!

Sally Shift Sally is always keen to maximise the gain of an expected big shift.

Sammy Soak Goes as low as he can downwind without losing velocity made good (vmg).

Samuel Sloppy Samuel is slow to round the leeward mark (he might get the mainsheet in too slowly for example) which means he has dirty wind (being leebowed by the boats in front).

Sarah Safe (Summer's sister) Sarah Safe doesn't risk tacking in front of a starboard boat but crosses to stay safe.

Scarlett Surf Scarlett likes to surf downwind and will always try and get to the best waves.

Sid Straight Line Sid is very good at taking account of current to ensure he always sails the minimum distance (a straight line) to the next mark of the course.

Sophie Starboard When Sophie is sailing upwind on starboard, and she sees a port tacker coming across, she just holds her course.

Summer Safe (Sarah's sister) Summer Safe tacks under a starboard boat to be safe.

Terry Tacker Terry tacks on the shifts so as to sail on the lifting tack.

Tilley Traffic Tilley avoids getting too close to other boats by staying away from the pack where possible.

Tyler Transit Tyler knows exactly where he is on the line as he has a good transit.

William Windy William is always off to the windiest part of the race course to help his boat go faster.

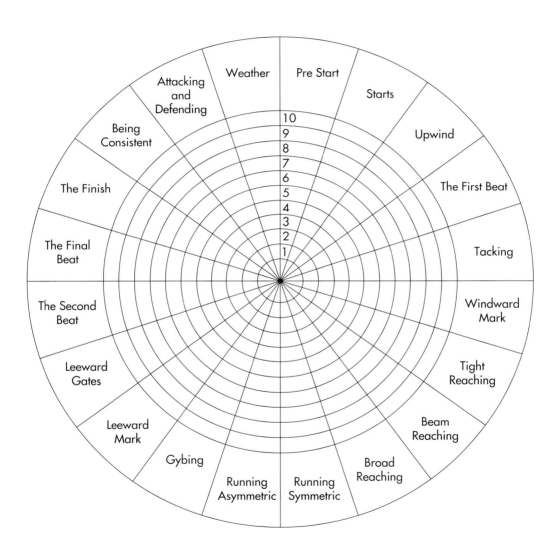

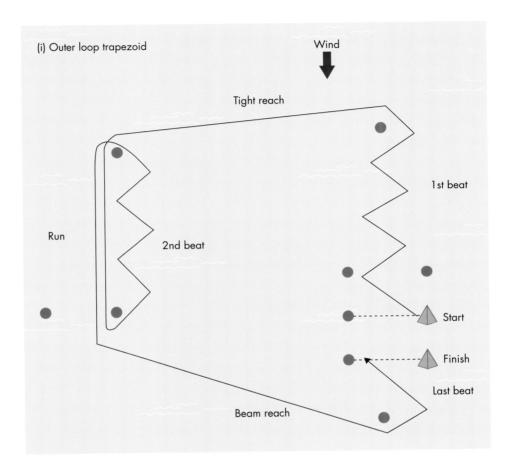

(i) Outer loop trapezoid

Wind

Tight reach

Run

2nd beat

1st beat

Start

Finish

Last beat

Beam reach

(ii) Inner loop trapezoid

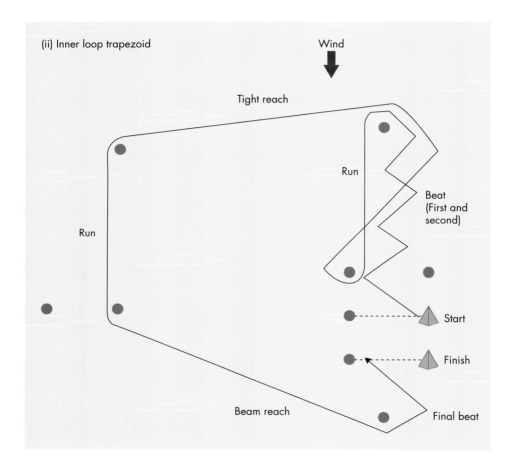

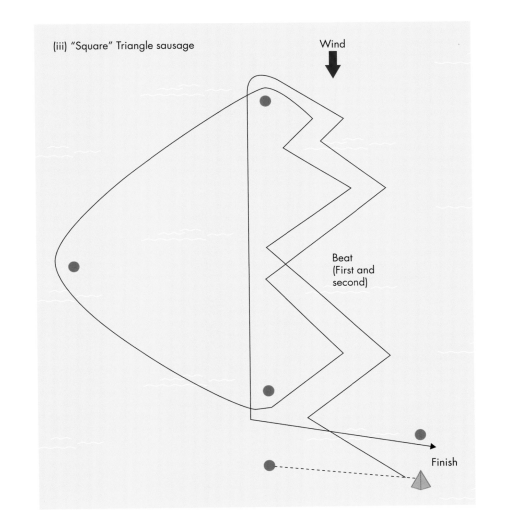

(iii) "Square" Triangle sausage

Wind

Beat
(First and
second)

Finish

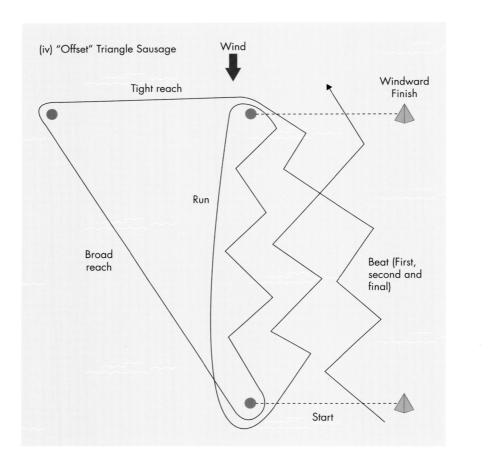

(iv) "Offset" Triangle Sausage

Wind

Tight reach

Windward Finish

Run

Broad reach

Beat (First, second and final)

Start